Narcissism in the Church

A Heart of Stone in Christian Relationships and Organizations

David C. Orrison PhD

D1714082

While the stories and illustrations used in this book are based on true events and compilations of real situations, the names and details have been fictionalized.

Scripture quotations are from *Holy Bible: The New King James Version*. 1982. Nashville: Thomas Nelson.

© David Orrison 2018 All Rights Reserved

No part of this book may be reproduced or transmitted in any form or by any means electronic or mechanical without written permission from the author except for brief quotations in critical articles and reviews.

Contents

Half of the harm that is done in this world

Is due to people who want to feel important

They don't mean to do harm

But the harm does not interest them.

Or they do not see it, or they justify it

Because they are absorbed in the endless struggle

To think well of themselves.

T. S. Eliot–The Cocktail Party

Introduction

A collection of symptoms consistently observed in an identifiable group of people.

That might be a reasonable definition of a disease. Over the last few decades, we have seen people struggle against patterns of symptoms for which there was no name. Because no known disease could be identified, some believed these struggles to be the effects of emotional or spiritual stresses. But as doctors realized there were groups of people suffering the same symptoms, they began to understand these were real and physical diseases. People who were accused of psychosomatic illnesses or deception finally found help and acceptance. Names of those diseases are now familiar to us, but victims endured ridicule and marginalization in the past. Their suffering was real even if not defined or accepted.

There is danger in naming an illness or a disorder. Professionals sometimes regret the resulting popular use of those names. Terms like "schizophrenia" and "influenza" have been both popular among laypeople and frustrating for professionals. People who are frightened of walking down a dark street are not necessarily "paranoid," according to the psychologist. Those who forget where they put their phones are not necessarily suffering from dementia. If you have a headache, you probably do not have the "flu." It can be less than helpful for those of us who are not professionals to use terms meant to be diagnostic and specific in popular ways.

At the same time, naming an illness brings legitimacy to a sufferer. Being able to say, "The doctor says I have *xyz*," removes the stigma of deception or emotional fabrication. Few things are more frightening than seeing the attacks of an unknown enemy. Naming the enemy allows the victim to build a structure, a picture, of what must be fought.

I have suffered migraines most of my life. When they first came, I thought I might have a brain tumor. Intense and localized pain indicated to me that something was very wrong. After several severe headaches, my parents took me to the doctor who said I had "classic migraine with aura." He even had some foul medicine I could take. The medicine didn't help and neither the pain nor the frequency lessened, but the peace of that simple word, "classic," told me things were not as wrong as I thought. There were others who suffered this. In fact, I later learned my grandmother had them. She didn't know what they were but called them her "sick headaches." I would also learn my father had a different version of migraine and that, yes, they were hereditary. From the moment the doctor named my problem, I had an enemy to fight. I could study, survey others, even experiment with prevention and treatment. Since that time, I have learned a great deal about my enemy—even how to control it.

I learned about narcissism in the church. Certain people seemed to have the ability to abuse others without remorse or consequence. They left discouragement and shame and brokenness behind them as they moved through relationships and churches. Victims knew something had happened, they felt the pain, but had no idea what it was. Some knew their persecutors, but still could not identify the behavior that caused such pain. When they tried to tell others about their suffering, they were doubted and rejected.

Over the years, I had seen this happen in organizational structures, in marriages, even in friendships. Positioning, manipulating, criticizing, shaming, lying—all symptoms that seemed to have no connection. These symptoms presented themselves consistently when certain people were active. Those symptoms revolved around the ones who seemed to cause the problems. Their victims also exhibited consistent symptoms:

confusion, rejection, defeat, fear, anger, and more. Yet, the differences in these situations and relationships revealed no common cause.

Then I sat in the bookstore reading about those who loved themselves at the expense of others. I discovered the term, "narcissism," and began to learn more about it. Finally, I had a name for what I was seeing. Finally, I had a focus for my study. When more and more of the symptoms, both in abusers and in victims, fit what I was seeing, I understood. Since that time, my use of this term for what I saw in the churches has been affirmed consistently.

I have been writing about narcissism for several years, through the ministry of *Grace for the Heart*, and I have taught classes on the subject. Over and over people have said, "I never knew what to call it, but it happened to me." They knew who was doing it. They knew how much it hurt. Yet, they didn't have a name. They felt like there was nothing they could do. Once they had a name, they had something they could fight.

Yes, the popular use of "narcissism" in our culture makes the professionals nervous. Perhaps it should. Defining a culture-wide behavior as a disorder should be disturbing. Many suggest narcissism is a behavioral problem rather than a disorder. Some say we have a cultural epidemic of narcissistic behavior. Wherever the truth lies, the term has been released to the public.

This book looks at narcissistic behavior in the church and within the families of the church. Of all places within the culture, the church would seem to be the antithesis of a welcoming place for narcissists. Yet, the symptoms of narcissistic behavior can be seen in Christian relationships every day. From the organization, to the families, to the communal relationships of members, the church may be every bit as affected by the narcissism of our culture as any group. Perhaps, in some ways, the church offers a haven for those who would abuse and use others.

The reader will not find an expose of Christian leaders here. Instead, the purpose will be an exposure of the common struggles of narcissism and how those struggles are found in church life. This is not a criticism of the church, but a simple attempt to show how even an institution supposedly dedicated to love and acceptance can be infected and affected by a most destructive disorder.

The problem centers on a narcissistic message pervading many churches. That message, as we will see, defines the culture of the church. It may be heard in the teaching, seen in the interactions, and felt in the criticisms and comparisons. The pastor may have established the message early in his ministry, or it might have come with a certain group of members, or it may even be a traditional part of denominational or sectarian culture. Whatever the source, the narcissistic message creates a system and enables participants within the church.

Throughout this book the gender of the narcissist will generally be masculine. The justification for this is the idea that the disorder is seen more in men. Occasionally, the "he/she" construct, or something similar will be used so the reader is reminded that both men and women can be narcissistic. The same is true when referring to church leadership. It should be obvious that both men and women lead the church, and both can exhibit abusive behaviors and attitudes.

The Narcissistic Message

Human beings are fundamentally isolated. We see only through our eyes. We think only our thoughts. Our ability to connect with others depends on our acceptance of them as persons like ourselves.

The old question asks whether a tree that falls in the forest makes a sound if no one is there to hear. The popularity of that question reveals our tenuous link between perception and reality. The "real world" consists of only what we can perceive in the present. To accept more than that is to accept a reality larger than ourselves, perhaps frighteningly larger.

Children, according to some, are born narcissistic. They have to learn to see others as separate persons rather than appendages. Perhaps the greatest shock of life is the separation every child experiences at birth. Suddenly, Mother comes and goes. Others enter the child's experience. The world of light and things and sensations must be nearly overwhelming. To understand it is filled with others who see through only their eyes and think only their thoughts takes a serious shift of worldview.

For the unborn, Mother is the source or supply. There is no awareness or acceptance of this. It is simply reality. When the child is born, the supply that is Mother becomes less available and less predictable. The child uses newly formed communication to demand the supply again. Sometimes others become that supply. Children struggle to control access to supply until they learn they can provide for themselves. They also must learn to control their desires until supply is available.

Most learn to embrace this strange world early. Children are forced to accept that Mother is not always immediately present and may not even instantly manifest when called. As we grow, we resign ourselves to that separation. Many professionals suggest that this process and time may be the source of psychological maladies that challenge us throughout life. Family dynamics and parental connection are significant factors in the development of the mind and heart of the child through this journey.

The fears of early childhood fade from our memories, but often imprint themselves on our souls. When Mother walks out of sight, does she still exist? How does the child know she will come back? If Mother exists out of sight, what else exists out of sight? Could there be a monster under the bed? Children develop their understanding of reality by reasoning through these questions. If they are guided by parents or others, and if they accept that guidance, they learn to trust and wait and look past their limited perceptions. But if parents are distant, or the child finds reasons to distrust the guidance given, then the ability to accept reality beyond perception is hindered.

This is, of course, a grossly oversimplified explanation of the key development process of the narcissistic mindset. Narcissism, in varying degrees, could be an unwillingness or inability to accept the reality of the world outside the person's perception. It certainly presents itself as difficulty accepting the reality and value of other persons.

Your identity matters only as you affect me

Narcissistic organizations and relationships share a common message to those on the "outside." That message centers on the lack of value and personhood of others. The narcissistic friend or parent or spouse sees others as having purpose and worth only in service to the narcissist. The narcissistic organization categorizes people by usefulness, either to the leadership or to the organization. The message becomes: "Your identity matters only as you affect me (or the organization)." That identity can be positive or negative, but never separate from the narcissistic entity.

So, the narcissistic mother abuses the privacy of her daughter because she sees no value in the separate identity of the child. The narcissistic boss requires unreasonable commitment because he sees nothing in the separate life of the employee. The narcissistic organization gives its people numbers and quotas and positions which ignore any sense of individuality apart from usefulness and conformity. The narcissistic friend is a friend only if he or she is being served.

Terms of relationship, like friend or daughter or co-worker, mean little to the narcissist. They must always be secondary to the person's value as servant. While this is difficult for people to hear, it explains much about the strange distance felt in the relationship. For the narcissist, there is little value in a person who is not useful. Relationships begin when usefulness is perceived and end when usefulness is completed. If one person's usefulness is greater than another's, the second person may be abandoned with no regret or responsibility felt by the narcissist. Thus, the boss can fire employees without compassion, the spouse can leave one partner for another, and the friend can simply move on. Even parents, when narcissistic, may choose to value one child over another or another child not at all.

More invasive or oppressive narcissists convince the people in their relationships that their identity has little substance apart from the narcissist. The value of the child lies in the contribution to the success of the family from the narcissist's perspective. The value of the spouse is determined only by service to the

Who are you apart from me?

narcissist. This appears to be true in all narcissistic relationships. The primary question from the narcissist is: Who are you apart from me? When the person walks out the door, the narcissist is barely aware of his/her continued existence. When the narcissist does assign value to a person, that person lives under nearly unreasonable scrutiny and accountability. Just as when Mother left the room and the infant screamed for her to return, the narcissist cannot allow the person to have an independent identity. Thus, the employee must always be on call, and the spouse must give account for mileage on the car.

Over time, this depersonalization may be accepted by the victim/supply. The wife may design her life around a narcissistic husband, with no outside interests or goals or support. The employee may have little life away from his job. The narcissist will, of course, cultivate this sacrifice. With no regard to the loss suffered, the narcissist will take more of the life energy, draining the one designated as "supply," until there is little or nothing left. Then the broken victim is discarded. The Assistant Manager has a nervous breakdown and is simply replaced by someone else.

The broken and incapable wife provides the narcissist with the opportunity to perform and accept attention as the burdened and victimized husband.

The victim is depersonalized in the narcissistic relationship. In the simplest sense, that means the narcissist does not see the other person as real and valid. Because the only value of others is in service to the narcissist, there is no reality, no person, apart from the narcissist. While this seems overstated, it explains a great deal of narcissistic behavior. Some narcissists play with their victims in ways reminiscent of cats playing with mice they intend to eat. Some seem to be able to abandon and forget employees, friends, organization members, even family members with no regret or explanation. The cruelties and distance of narcissism come out of this depersonalization.

At the same time, the narcissist is quite aware of "the system." While people may not exist the way the narcissist does, they do exist in the system, and the system exists. From the earliest years, the narcissist has been aware that there is something outside himself, something that affects supply. Life has been a process of manipulating that system. Sometimes he fails at making the system work for him, and he becomes the victim. Other times he "works" the system to serve him, and he is the victor.

People in narcissistic relationships will often hear their narcissist say things like: "Everything is against me." That "everything" is the nameless and faceless system. Or: "You just have to know how it's done." Here the narcissist suggests he knows how to manipulate the system. For a time, he has become superior to the system. The system is impersonal, arbitrary, and malevolent. Like a great beast one must either fear or conquer, the system offers the primary challenge to the narcissist's life.

Other people are manifestations of the system. Narcissists typically categorize people according to the type of connection within the system. Others may be support for the narcissist, opposition for the narcissist, or (at the present) of no consequence to the narcissist. Those who are supportive are to be used. Those who oppose are to be overcome or destroyed. Those who do not affect the narcissist either way may be ignored or watched in case they eventually lean toward support or opposition.

So, narcissists will interact with people in a wide variety of ways. We should not expect the narcissist to walk through life as a disaffected loner. Instead, the narcissist gives to and receives from others as though they were characters in a complex role-playing game. He may even become attached to one character or another, find that person so useful and dependable that the loss of the person is emotionally negative. He may hate certain characters, attack them without mercy or hesitation simply because of his emotions. He will invest in some relationships with acts of kindness and generosity. He will also cruelly use others without remorse. And, for the most part, when one character is taken away or becomes less useful, he will simply pick up with another.

> **The narcissist does not consider the benefit of his kindness nor the damage of his cruelty, except as it serves his purposes**

On the surface, this appears the same as normal relationships, although somewhat cruel and self-serving. But, for the narcissist, "real" relationships are as artificial as those with fictional characters. Love and hate, kindness and cruelty, are simply part of the game. The game exists to supply the narcissist with self-affirmation. We must not assume the narcissist is altruistic. Nor is he hateful toward those who oppose him. He is simply self-serving. The narcissist does not consider the benefit of his kindness nor the damage of his cruelty, except as it serves his purposes. There can be no real effect on the characters of the system if they are not real in the same sense the narcissist is real. There is no love the way the rest of us speak of love, nor is there hate.

This is the underlying message of the narcissist to the people in his/her life:

You are not real to me. You do not exist except as you interact with me. Your value hinges on how you affect me. I cannot love you or hate you. I can only use you. If you oppose me, I must delete you. If you serve me, my way, I will treat you as though you have value. Your purpose is to reflect to me what I want to see in myself.

Most people who finally hear the clear message of narcissism find it to be shocking. Normal people do not function or think like that. In fact, we tend to assume other people think like we do. We learned others are real and have value apart from us. We may not fully appreciate or understand that reality, but we accept it. When we encounter someone who uses and manipulates and categorizes people in the same way they would tools or objects, we find it very difficult to relate. That same difficulty is felt by the narcissist trying to understand why the rest of us are so offended and hurt by his actions. If he accepts that others are real at all, he expects we think like him.

So why would anyone be attracted to such a person? Because we need the same thing. We want the narcissist to tell us who we are. We learn about ourselves as we relate to others. Other people are the mirrors by which our behavior and other attributes are reflected back to us. Children learn about themselves as they bounce ideas and actions off the sensibilities of others. When we grow up in a community of others, we develop our identity. But we get mixed messages from people who are also trying to see themselves in us. We don't know if they are reflecting a true image back, or if they may be showing us something of themselves. Until we are able to accept that our identity will not come from these reflections, we tend to bounce from feeling good about ourselves to feeling inferior and unworthy.

When we meet a narcissist, we often find someone immediately attractive. When a narcissist cultivates a relationship, he is friendly, strong, and likable. In his eyes, we want to see ourselves. But the narcissist understands this need. He reflects to us what we want to believe. Narcissists are almost always great listeners and affirming heroes as the relationship begins. They communicate acceptance and value to us through their words, body language, and presence. By projecting strength and confidence, the narcissist draws people into relationship, causing them to believe they are loved and full of promise. In a sense, the narcissist shows us a little of himself: his vision of success and superiority. As we learn of him, we find hope for ourselves. We like his strength. We like his charisma. We feel good as we associate ourselves with him.

At the beginning, we may not understand how the narcissist is training us to feed his image of himself back to him. It happens naturally. The narcissist feels good about the relationship and so do we. Later, if we get to know him better, we will begin to see the normal flaws of any human. The narcissist, however, cannot accept that we see these flaws. If the relationship continues, he will begin to manipulate or control to get the attention, obedience, and service he wants.

All of this is easier with people who are already prepared to think of themselves as inferior, unworthy, and in need of guidance. Narcissists look for people who feel undervalued and both hate and accept that status. The ideal relationship, for the narcissist, is one in which the person is benefited as he/she lifts up the narcissist. In other words, you feel better about yourself as you admire and serve the narcissist.

It would be difficult to find a more ideal and prepared group of people for this kind of narcissistic relationship than members in most churches. Although it can be hard to admit, most people in church have been trained to think of themselves as failures, unworthy of kindness and attention. Focus on sin, servant status, and inability cultivate a longing for affirmation in the hearts of church people. Narcissists use those feelings to elevate themselves.

The Old Story

Many generations ago, in the nearly forgotten times, there were two young people bound by their own needs. One was the nymph named Echo. Echo loved to talk. She longed for a lasting relationship with someone who valued her. She extended every conversation by adding one more comment, thus pulling the person more and more into a relationship with her. One day Echo began a conversation with a beautiful woman. Frustrated by the girl's need to have the last word, the beautiful woman (who was really the goddess Juno) placed a curse on Echo. She would have the last word of every conversation, but never the first; and her last words would always be the last words of the person with whom she was talking.

Soon, Echo was driven to the woods and hills to escape relationships. She despaired of love and acceptance. But then she found the young man named Narcissus. Narcissus moved with the grace and assurance of a young god. He was beautiful to look at, and all people loved him. They had showered him with praises from the time of his birth. Echo fell in love with Narcissus.

Narcissus loved no one. When Echo reached out to him, she was able only to speak his own last few words back to him. A conversation ensued, and Echo believed there was hope for a relationship. But Narcissus did not enjoy the sound of his own words. Their stark honesty made him bitter against Echo, and he pushed her away. With a broken heart, Echo retreated to the caves and hills again. No one has seen her since.

Narcissus continued his life, never opening his heart to another, rejecting all who came to love him, until the day his own curse came to its fruit. He stopped at a pool where the water was perfectly still, and he looked at his own reflection. Suddenly, Narcissus was in love. No one had been so beautiful, so full of promise, so wonderful in potential. For the first and only time in his life, Narcissus found a relationship he would enjoy.

No matter how others urged him, Narcissus would not leave the pool. From time to time he reached out to embrace his image, but the water stirred, and the image was lost. Forever just out of reach, the image called to him and captured his heart. Finally, one day people noticed that Narcissus no longer leaned over the little pool. He was gone. In his place stood a beautiful white flower which has forever borne his name.

So, there you have it—the story of Narcissus and Echo. Those ancient storytellers understood human nature in ways we are just beginning to reclaim. The classic narcissist and his classic victim captured in a tale told to children for millennia. The story has different versions and is told with different emphases, but the message continues to explain what so many see today.

What Is Narcissism?

A list of behavioral tendencies is used to diagnose narcissism. People can be found on a spectrum of actions and attitudes that define narcissism. This is true for either a professional diagnosis or a lay diagnosis. Obviously, each will have its uses. Those who are higher on the list, exhibiting more characteristics, may be said to be narcissists.

A narcissistic organization or system (or message) is usually designed to serve one or more narcissists as they work to achieve recognition and power corresponding to their perceived superiority. The narcissistic CEO creates a system which both feeds his/her need for affirmation and continually brings new sources of supply. At every level of the company, in his perfect world, the workers will look up to and long to be him. The narcissistic pastor creates a church in much the same manner. The members will worship and obey.

However, the narcissistic system can survive after the narcissist moves on. As we will see, once the system is in place, it attracts narcissists. Those who need others to affirm their image of superiority will find a ready supply in the church. So, with or without the pastor, narcissism can become the culture of the church.

Before we go much further, however, let's give a general definition of narcissism. You will find two diagnostic tools below, but here are three basic parts of the narcissistic structure. When these three parts are in place, the structure is firm.

1. The superior image

2. Depersonalization of others

3. Use and abuse of others to serve the image

I would suggest that all of these are necessary to establish the presence of narcissism.

First, the general professional opinion is that narcissists fear what they perceive as reality. Perhaps from some childhood trauma or abandonment, they learned they were not acceptable. The rejection and loss they experienced because of this accumulated over time, and they could find no way out. In their despair and fear, they decided to create an image, a golem of themselves, that was better than others. This image could not be rejected or ignored. Because of the intense personal investment in this image and the young age when it was created, the adult narcissist barely remembers the image is not real. Instead, the narcissist presents himself/herself as superior, as identical with the image.

This image takes a great deal of energy to support. The child learns how to manipulate the people and situations of his life to support that image. For example, the young boy wants others to see him as superior in all things, including sports. Rather than learn how to be superior in all sports, he must learn how to make others see something that isn't there. When the guys get together to throw the football, he can fake a shoulder injury from the last time he threw, then tell a story about how well he threw the ball. Or, if he tries to throw and fails, he can blame others, or the wind, or whatever. Something or someone else is responsible for his failure. If he throws the ball and succeeds, he probably will not try again. He will find throwing the football boring and encourage the others toward some other activity. Or he may begin to criticize others, lifting their failures to the front. In all these ways, he believes he is establishing his superior abilities. All that is important is that the other boys believe he could throw better than any of them if he wanted to. By the time the narcissist is an adult, he/she has learned how to manipulate what others think.

Second, because the pain of rejection always comes from other people, the child begins to depersonalize those around him. This means he takes away their value as real persons in his life. Instead, they become useful according to their category. Some people will be tools used to accomplish goals. Others will be toys to enjoy along the way. Still others will be obstacles to goals. Some may even be ignored as unworthy of any attention. None are real persons.

Depersonalization is necessary for the narcissist. Others have hurt him/her and may bring that pain again. It is better to stay separate from others. What better way to stay separate than to wipe away personhood from everyone? If no one is real, then no one can cause real pain. Criticisms and expectations can be ignored. Anyone who opposes the narcissist can be destroyed without regret. Anyone who adores the image can be exploited without regret. After all, what carpenter becomes emotional over the impact of a hammer on a nail? If people are tools to serve in reaching goals, then what happens to them does not matter.

Lack of empathy is a defining characteristic of narcissism. Because others are not real persons, the narcissist cannot/will not connect with their feelings. He may learn how to respond at certain times, for the purpose of reaching his own goals, but he will not care. He/she will offer condolences, sympathy, congratulations according to what he/she has learned, but will not have the connection others expect. This inability to empathize serves the narcissist well. There is no hesitation to treat people according to their category. Obstacles are meant to be overcome, even destroyed. Toys are meant to be enjoyed, then discarded. Tools serve the purpose for which they were chosen. This is why narcissistic bosses can fire, promote, overuse employees without concern. The broken heart of an abandoned spouse means nothing to the narcissist, unless that spouse decides to become an obstacle to further goals.

Finally, the third leg of the narcissism structure puts the first two into action. Not only does the narcissist have a superior image to maintain. Not only does the narcissist not see others as real people. The narcissist will use and abuse anyone to serve that superior image. Perhaps this is obvious, but if the narcissist does not hurt others, there is no reason to consider his perspective a problem for the rest of us. He may be lying to himself, but if his lies don't affect others, it may not matter. The fact that a narcissist follows through on using others to serve the image creates the societal dysfunction that causes concern.

But, of course, narcissists are abusers. Perhaps not physical or sexual abusers, but they do abuse. I usually say almost all physical and sexual abusers are narcissists, but not all narcissists treat their victims that way. Abuse can be far more subtle. Constant criticism, compromised praise, capitalizing on weaknesses—these are abusive. Stealing, lying, and manipulating can be abusive. Narcissists use others to accomplish their purpose, to maintain or build the image. If those others are hurt along the way, the narcissist doesn't care.

This is an important point about narcissistic abuse: it rarely is personal. It may feel personal, directed and intimate, but it simply serves the purpose of the narcissist. Rather than attack you as a person, the narcissist attacks you as an obstacle. The depth of your destruction depends on the size of the obstacle you represent. Or the

Narcissistic abuse is rarely personal

narcissist attacks you as a tool, to move you to some action. Like the violence of the file as it sharpens the ax, the narcissist does whatever he feels necessary to make you function the way he wants. Or the narcissist attacks you as a toy. The dog may destroy the toy just because it feels good, not because it hates the toy. The narcissist may attack you because it makes him/her feel better. Tearing you down may simply be a way of lifting the narcissist up. But it isn't about you.

I understand that brings little comfort and may even seem hard to believe. Understanding the motivation of narcissistic abuse is particularly challenging to those who can't imagine abusing anyone. In fact, trying to make sense of any narcissistic action or thinking is almost impossible for those who are not narcissists.

Now, I have already been freer with the term, "narcissist," than I should be, according to most professionals. Words have meanings, they say. To use a clinical term for undiagnosed people borders on inappropriate. I don't disagree. We must deal with the conflict between the clinical use and the popular use of this term.

For psychological and counseling professionals, narcissism is a clinical diagnosis with specific symptoms and various methods of treatments. It proves to be particularly difficult to diagnose, and treatment is often discontinued or fruitless. At best, narcissists can be trained to conform better in society and treat others with respect. At worst, the narcissist laughs off the diagnosis and believes the now-popular word to be an affirmation of superiority.

Narcissism is considered a "Cluster B" personality disorder, classified with Borderline, Antisocial, and Histrionic. The following summary is from the *Diagnostic and Statistical*

Manual of Mental Disorders Fourth edition (DSM IV). I prefer it over the revision of the DSM V, although the wording of the descriptions has changed minimally. It is presented as quoted in *The Wizard of Oz and Other Narcissists*, by Eleanor D. Payson (2002, page 21).

"A pervasive pattern of grandiosity (in fantasy or behavior), need for admiration, and lack of empathy, beginning by early adulthood and present in a variety of contexts, as indicated by five (or more) of the following:

1. has a grandiose sense of self-importance (e.g., exaggerates achievements and talents, expects to be recognized as superior without commensurate achievements).

2. is preoccupied with fantasies of unlimited success, power, brilliance, beauty, or ideal love.

3. believes that he or she is "special" and unique and can only be understood by, or should associate with, other special or high status people (or institutions).

4. requires excessive admiration.

5. has a sense of entitlement, i.e., unreasonable expectations of especially favorable treatment or automatic compliance with his or her expectations.

6. is interpersonally exploitative, i.e., takes advantage of others to achieve his or her own ends.

7. lacks empathy: is unwilling to recognize or identify with the feelings and needs of others

8. is often envious of others or believes that others are envious of him or her.

9. shows arrogant, haughty behaviors or attitudes."

A professional diagnosis of narcissism is difficult to achieve, except for extreme cases. This is partly because the diagnostic tool would seem to require only extreme extensions of the listed behaviors and beliefs. Otherwise, many people would be diagnosed as narcissists. It is also because narcissists are deceptive, smart enough and willing to adapt answers to questions to avoid an undesirable diagnosis. The wife who can get her narcissistic husband to attend a counseling session will probably see a radical adjustment of personality while with the therapist. Many have reported that the counselor believed the abuser, rather than the victim, because of the persuasiveness of the personality.

*****

So how does a victim get a handle on the cause of the abuse in his/her life? When a person exhibits some of these traits, without a clinical diagnosis, can others say that person is a narcissist? Yes, but in a looser sense. In a medical sense, saying you had the "flu" last week might not be right. Unless you went to the doctor and received a professional diagnosis, you only observed certain symptoms in yourself that others have called the flu. The term has become popular, changing from "influenza" to "flu." But many or most of the symptoms are the same and the term still denotes a communicable illness with fever, muscle aches, and respiratory symptoms. And when you say the flu is going around, you may not mean an official epidemic; you may simply be telling your friend to wash his hands more carefully, so he doesn't get the same symptoms. Because we don't usually have easy access to professional diagnoses, we generalize the meanings of words. There is significant value in this if we remember that terms like influenza and narcissism have clinical applications and we are not using those terms in that way.

For those who deal with narcissistic people at home, at work, or at church, narcissism is a source of pain and confusion. With or without a professional diagnosis, a person or group causes that suffering. While there may be unfortunate aspects to a clinical term becoming popularized, narcissism has developed a popular and useful meaning. That popular use could become detrimental if separated from the clinical use altogether, however.

Magazines and web sources have developed many self-diagnostic tools over the past few years, basically "You Might Be a Narcissist If…" tests. The problem is that normal people, who aren't narcissists, take the tests and discover narcissistic behaviors in themselves. In a guilt-ridden society (or a blame and shame church culture, which we will talk about later), many will add narcissism to their list of self-condemnations. Meanwhile, true narcissists either would not take the popular test or would laugh to find themselves and their behaviors.

Those who suspect they are in a relationship with a narcissist can look at the professional diagnostic tool above and temper it by the list below. Again, multiple symptoms would be required to suggest narcissism. To remind us that narcissists can be either male or female, the list uses both.

He or she might be narcissistic if:

1. He cannot bear to lose an argument. She will change the discussion, the subject, the rules. He will become angry, threatening, demeaning, etc. She simply cannot be wrong unless it is someone else's fault.

2. She has no sense of your personal boundaries. What's hers is hers and what's yours is hers. He sits at your desk, uses your things, and may even touch you in unwelcome ways.

3. After working with him on a project, you feel used. She takes credit for what you do. The more you work with him, the more you realize he doesn't do as much as you thought.

4. He talks about himself all the time, yet you don't really feel like you know him. She never asks how you are or about things that are important to you. It's all about her.

5. He is full of big stories that make him look good, but his boasts don't match what you see at work. She has all kinds of great plans and her schedule is full, but you don't see her doing anything significant.

6. He is often angry, especially with others who don't do what he thinks they should. She claims to be the victim of abuses of others, but you haven't seen them being mean to her.

7. His words and his behavior are quite different. He ridicules and derides others, then does the same thing himself. She knows unkind information about everyone but can't seem to remember important or simple things about them.

8. He believes he is better than others, particularly bosses and other leaders. Yet, he never expresses this to them. She thinks others envy her and judge her unfairly, yet she does the same thing.

9. She expects you to notice her hair or clothing, but never comments positively on yours unless she wants you to do something for her. He shows off his watch, his car, his wife, or something, and has no interest in yours. His kids are the greatest at everything, and he has no idea whether you have kids.

10. He has no qualms about calling you at inconvenient times to ask you to do difficult or inappropriate things for him. He shows up to help you just as the job is finishing, then acts like he was helping all along. She is very good at volunteering for a job and then getting you or someone else to do it for her, perhaps begging off at the last minute with some lame excuse.

To summarize, and give a practical definition of narcissism, use this statement: *Narcissism depersonalizes others and categorizes them according to usefulness in serving an image of superiority.* Narcissists use others without regard to suffering in supporting this image. This can be true for a person or an organization. No one is more important than that image. The narcissist is better than anyone else. The narcissistic organization is better than all others. All relationships are designed to serve this one purpose. All energy is spent to maintain the perceived superiority.

The Story of First Church

First Church, Eastview, began when Pastor Jenkins left his position as Associate Pastor in the city. He and the Senior Pastor didn't agree on a few things. Pastor Jenkins knew he could do better on his own. He had dreams and goals and believed himself of a quality that could make a church grow. When the suburb began to grow and developed its own retail area, Pastor Jenkins believed it could support a church. He began to talk with church members who supported him in his desires to "do more for God." His supporters encouraged him to use his gifts in greater ways than just as an Associate Pastor.

The day came when Pastor Jenkins went to the Senior Pastor and said he would be starting a new church in Eastview. He already had a few dozen people from the city church who lived in that direction and wanted to go with him. He had also talked with denominational officials about the desirability of a church plant in that area. Unofficially, they agreed that his knowledge of the area and connections with the people would be a great way to start the new church. Officially, they said he needed the blessing of the Senior Pastor.

So, Pastor Jenkins offered the Senior Pastor a choice: the city church could split, and some would start a new church in Eastview, or the Senior Pastor could convince the elders and the congregation to support a new daughter church in Eastview, planted by Pastor Jenkins. With the support of the denomination, the Senior Pastor chose the latter.

From the beginning, it was clear that First Church belonged to Pastor Jenkins. He chose the leaders. He set the standards. He managed the corporation. Everything was according to denominational polity, of course. Yet, everything was arranged and approved by Pastor Jenkins.

Eastview did grow, and so did First Church. Soon First Church rivaled the city church in numbers. Pastor Jenkins was a rising star in the denomination. First Church was a model for successful church planting. It wasn't long before denominational headquarters asked Pastor Jenkins to come and lead their church planting program.

What no one saw, of course, was the controlling hand of Pastor Jenkins. Only those he deemed competent and submissive could lead in the church. There were some who wanted to lead in a growing ministry. Others wanted to be closer to Pastor Jenkins as he rose in popularity. Still others simply wanted to help. But not everyone was allowed to lead.

Because of the growth of the town, new people were always visiting, and no one noticed how many left the church. As long as the growth rate excelled that of normal churches, Pastor Jenkins continued to be a hero. When anyone pointed out that some attenders were missing, he would point to all the new members. Church plants always have a wide-open back door, Pastor Jenkins said. People come and go, he said.

When Pastor Jenkins left First Church, it was difficult to find someone to replace him. A couple of the Associate Pastors thought they should have the job, but the elders were particularly loyal to Pastor Jenkins and believed the associates to be lesser servants. For the next few months, the elder team, led by Mr. Dennis, held the church together and kept it on the track set by the pastor. Mr. Dennis allowed no dissension in the team. Any elders who disagreed with his leadership were encouraged to step down. In this time of "stressful transition," he said, the elders should be unified. That meant they should do what he said… just as they had done what Pastor Jenkins said.

Mr. Dennis wanted a pastor who would bring the church back to Biblical standards. The only criticism he had of Pastor Jenkins was that the pastor had focused more on building the membership than on preaching the Bible. That philosophy brought people in, now they should be taught truth, he said. A lot of the people in the church were not living up to God's standards, Mr. Dennis said.

Eventually, the elder team brought in Pastor Harlen to lead the church. Pastor Harlen was one of the most conservative ministers in the denomination and had a strong preaching style. Some people left the church because of the new preaching message, but new people continued to come. If the numbers in the church slipped a little, that could be attributed to the loss of Pastor Jenkins. If the numbers slipped a lot, the church was simply being purified.

As things turned out, the numbers of First Church plateaued about the same time as the numbers in the suburb. The church never regained the status it had during Pastor Jenkins' tenure, but everyone understood that. It was still a healthy congregation, most believed. Those who wanted to leave did so. Those who stayed agreed with the message and the system.

Why the Church?

Somewhere in history, churches began referring to members as "giving units" or "attenders" rather than people. They started to count heads on Sundays and names on membership lists. Growth no longer had a spiritual meaning but focused on numbers. At conferences and denominational gatherings, pastors were asked about the growth of their churches. Everyone had to have some explanation for growth or loss, because numbers became the measure of success. "Bodies, buildings, and bucks!" was the new battle cry.

The word "pastor" lost its meaning of "shepherd" in favor of "manager." The preacher became a teacher. The team of elders became a "board." Denominations received "per capita taxes" (head tax, based on member numbers) from each church to support organizational work. Boards of trustees managed campuses and budgets and staff and corporation legalities.

Perhaps none of this was wrong. Perhaps it was the natural process for the church in today's world. Perhaps churches will grow out of this process. Rather than judge the changes, we should see the attraction they bring to narcissists.

The narcissistic message needs two things to function in an organization or family. First, it needs hierarchy. However, the hierarchy is expressed—officially or subtly, politically or spiritually—it serves to categorize the members. Each person in the group knows his or her place. Assignment of that place usually comes after some type of examination and tenure within the group.

The narcissistic message needs hierarchy and control

The second thing the message needs is control. Hierarchy suggests control but doesn't demand it. Free people can disregard the desires of their leaders. There must be some way for narcissistic leadership to cause people to do what they want. That could be through direct coercion, or it could be through gentler means, like manipulation or indoctrination.

The church provides both of these to people who are unusually ready to bear them. Think about this from a marketing standpoint. The church is an "opt-in" connection for most people. That means they choose to be there. We live in a day when most adults do not have to go to church. So, they go because they are seeking something, something they hope the church can give them. There is at least a part of each person that wants to submit and find the answers.

When you get in the car and drive to the store because you need something, how hard is it for the salesman to sell it to you? Not hard, right? In fact, sometimes they must work to get you out of the store without the item you came for. If you can't find the item, you ask and follow directions. You'll search, because you believe the store has it… and you want it.

This is what is meant by an "opt-in" connection. You choose to go to that store. You want something you think they have. In the same way, people choose to attend church services. They feel a need in their hearts and think the church may offer a solution for that need. They come ready to listen and learn, ready to try.

Sadly, just like those who come with money in hand to buy are easy marks for the unscrupulous salesman, people who come to church with obvious needs easily become prey for narcissistic church leaders. Because the church member wants the leader to provide answers and guidance, he or she will be more open to that influence than in other areas of life.

Add to that the church's overall message about members being kind, forgiving, and obedient. We are called to right living, and that generally means a gentle and gracious walk. Gentle and dependent sheep are easier to control.

And, again, this has nothing to do with the type of church. People come to church, whatever kind it is, for help and community, things they need in their lives. If that church promises to provide those things, the people will stay. They will also be much more likely to submit to whatever hierarchical structure and control is said to be necessary.

Once the hierarchy and opportunity for control is in place, there are a few extras the narcissist would love to have. These are not necessary but make the church much more attractive.

The church offers a surprising lack of accountability for its leaders. The higher the leader, the less the accountability. In general, pastors set their own hours, their own goals, and their own standards for achievement. The idea that the pastor's job is difficult for others to examine or evaluate has been very helpful for those who want their freedom in that job. Most pastors have only a denominational structure in authority above them, one particularly susceptible to politics and apathy.

As I write this, I find myself defending these facts. I do not deny that a certain freedom is right for the pastor's job. My point is simply that it makes abuse easier. A lack of accountability allows the leader flexibility to focus where he/she wants to focus.

Some pastors might object that the job of trying to please all the people is not without accountability. But narcissists would not feel that pressure. The people don't matter to them. They would view the people as those whose need makes them weak and of less value. What right would the people have to tell the leader how to do his job? That would be the question of the narcissist.

The church also has a vague definition of success or even progress. How good is good enough for God? Many churches look to the Bible for that guidance, but the Bible doesn't give us a measurement for success. Is keeping the Ten Commandments enough? Jesus had to address that for the Pharisees and other Jewish leaders. He said hating your brother was tantamount to murder. Yet, the Pharisees were not content with other commandments. They added nuances and additional rules and demanded obedience.

The Bible was never interested in measuring behavior to find adequate levels. The Bible forces us to realize that anything less than perfection means we need a Savior. In the narcissistic system, blame can be assigned to anyone who is not perfect. That allows the leadership, or the organization, to shame everyone and to expect submission to teaching and expectations.

If perfection is impossible, and that is the only standard for true success, then what is "good enough"? What does practical success look like if true success is impossible? Narcissistic leaders may set their own standards for members, and/or keep members striving without end.

The church also tolerates inadequate, or at least controlled, communication. Church leaders often consider their call to ministry as being "set apart" for a different work than that of regular church members. The narcissist understands that to mean "superior." Those who are inferior are to trust and obey the leaders. After all, church leadership is appointed by God.

That superiority makes communication less necessary. That means board meetings may be closed. Committees may not have to report to the congregation. Transparency in handling money, setting goals, and staff relations may satisfy only legal requirements (and sometimes not even that).

In a culture without open communication, narcissists can and will do as they please. They can report decisions rather than discuss them. Agendas may not allow input from members. Members may be discouraged from seeking information that could threaten the freedom or authority of the leaders. Those who persist will be marginalized or disciplined.

Most members tolerate this. They didn't come to the church to make decisions. They came for the help they thought they needed. If they still believe that help is out there, they will be content to allow leadership to do as they will.

So, the church offers a cornucopia of delights for the narcissist. We should not be surprised that the narcissist is drawn to the church. Nor should we be surprised the members allow that kind of leadership, particularly once they are in the system and hearing the message.

If we look back to the definition of narcissism and remember the three requirements for a narcissistic culture, we can see that those requirements are met easily in most churches.

1. The superior image

2. Depersonalization of others

3. Use and abuse of others to serve the image

The superior image is almost inherent in the church culture. With a call to "be like Jesus," who could ever measure up? The desire to promote the image becomes a process of comparison, as we will see later. Even churches without that focus support a hierarchy both political and spiritual. Those who do well are rewarded and recognized as though they are farther on the path toward conformity to the image. Those chosen to lead are also viewed as closer to the image. The image, even if human based, is always present.

No one likes to think people are depersonalized at church. Yet, when families are called "giving units," and no one cares about those who leave, depersonalization is happening. To depersonalize does not mean to devalue. It means to treat as a unit, a member, rather than a real person with unique gifts and needs. It means the pastor looks out on the congregation to see the image based on numbers or performance, rather than the individuals.

Sadly, many have discovered that the church offers an excellent culture for abuse. When the image is central, those who do not benefit that image can be sacrificed or manipulated. Abuse is covered for the sake of the image or even sanctioned. The narcissistic person or organization does not care about victims, but about the image.

The Story of Faith Church

Bill says he doesn't feel like he has been to church unless he comes out of the service feeling guilty and ashamed. Sally appreciates Pastor Greg so much. He tells her what she is doing wrong and helps her get back on track. Mike says he learns something new about his failures every Sunday. Judy listens to the sermons several times during the week, so she can "get it right."

People dress up to attend Faith Church. Pastor Greg says God does not look on the outward appearance, but the outward reflects the inward. Most people speak quietly and act responsibly. Even the children are well-behaved. Pastor Greg says no one is judged at his church, but God is always watching.

Someone asked Frank how he would sum up the ministry of Faith Church. He suggested one word: character. Then he said the people at Faith Church are learning to measure up to the standards God has set for them. He has been very grateful for Pastor Greg's consistent focus on what it means to be Christian. He agrees there is too much compromise in the church today.

If you were to visit Faith Church, you would find friendly people, enthusiastic worship, and a strong message. You would be impressed with the power and authority of the sermon. After the service, Pastor Greg would meet you at the door. He would be gracious and caring. You would tell him where you live, why you have visited, and what church you used to attend. Something would make you feel like you should apologize, perhaps for your former church affiliation or for your kids who didn't want to come. But Pastor Greg would not chastise you. He would sympathize. He may even offer to talk with you, explaining how Faith Church offers a difference for your family.

As you leave Faith Church, you would be impressed with the orderliness and diligence you experienced. Most of all, you would be impressed with Pastor Greg. He looked you in the eye and shook your hand firmly and warmly. There was no compromise in his message or weakness in his character. You might say Faith Church had something special, something you had not experienced in other churches, but you probably **Everything at Faith Church was better** wouldn't be able to say much more than the word you picked up somehow: character. Pastor Greg and the people of Faith Church certainly valued character.

But even after that first visit, you might find yourself comparing. You compare yourself to the people you saw at Faith Church. They were well-dressed. The children were well-behaved. The women smiled, the men stood tall, the pastor spoke with confidence. Another word would slip into your thinking: better. Although you probably wouldn't express it that way yet, everything at Faith Church was better, of better character. The church was better than other churches. The people were better than you. The families were better than yours. The music, the building, the character—it was all better. If you were to stop to reason this out (which you almost certainly would not do) you probably wouldn't be able to say where the idea of better came from. Somehow—through the message, the songs, the comments—somehow a comparison system was set up in your mind, and your place was near the bottom. At least that's how you felt.

Years later, as a member of Faith Church, you might try to think back to what attracted you to the church in the first place. You might realize they offered something, something you felt you needed. Help with your family or marriage. Help with your relationship with God. There was something that dangled in front of you like the carrot on the stick urging you forward. But you might realize that all the Bible studies, all the sermons, all the special prayer events, all your participation didn't give you what you were looking for.

Manipulating the Message

Narcissism is about control. Some people come to church looking for that control. They may not want to admit their desire, but the world and the responsibilities of life make them afraid. They want a handle on things. They want to know how to guarantee the results they desire.

If there is one consistent characteristic of narcissistic leaders, it must be confidence. Feelings of superiority project to others as strength and self-assurance. In a day of confusion and ever-changing "truth," that strength and assurance offer hope. The narcissistic leader personifies what many people think they need in their lives. He/she can make decisions without hesitation. He/she can face objections and challenges and win. The narcissist exhibits personal peace and satisfaction, at least to those who are not close. For frightened parents, wearied

The narcissistic leader personifies what many people think they need in their lives

workers, and suffering victims, the promise and evidence of success surmount many of life's normal cautions.

The distinction between clergy and laypeople has served narcissists for many centuries. Remaining separate from the people, while controlling them, fits well in the narcissistic pattern. In other relationships, the narcissist must assert and affirm superiority to avoid challenges and control the inferiors. In the church, however, leaders twist Scriptural teachings of service into establishment of position. While the Master showed His greatness by washing feet and caring for the needy, the narcissist leader becomes great by virtue of his position. While Jesus established a close and loving relationship with the people He met, the narcissist leader distances himself from the people in order to cultivate that sense of superiority.

The narcissist must remain separate from the people. The closer the relationship is, the less the narcissist can cover his/her disdain for the people and the weakness he/she feels with intimacy. In almost any narcissistic relationship, familiarity truly does breed contempt. Those who hear the side comments and the more private thoughts of the narcissist experience the negative of that relationship.

In the church, the leader has two ways in which to become insulated against the people. Some create staff positions

Narcissism in the Church

designed to act as barriers. Many senior pastors today see few of their people, and the people have been conditioned to accept this as normal. Any recognition before or after the service, any special note from the pastor (no matter which secretary prepared it), will be considered favor from the one "on high."

But another way for the narcissist to separate from the people is to be considered better. For years, those in ministry have talked about the "pedestal" on which the pastor stands, whether by his own choice or by the choice of the people. That pedestal has not disappeared. Leadership in some churches is a progressive climb to the pedestal. Those who lead are honored according to the step they are on. They are also seen as progressively more spiritual or holy, according to whatever traditions the church holds. To be more spiritual, at least in the eyes of the narcissist, is to be better. To be better is to be superior and, therefore, separate.

The narcissist has a significant interest in a system that allows this kind of separation and spiritual hierarchy. How can the narcissistic church leader keep that system working? By adapting the message of the church so that it feeds the system. Fortunately for the narcissist, many churches already have a message that comes close.

Remember the goal: to control others so that the narcissist is protected and superior. Many narcissists do not seek accolades or the spotlight, but they still need to feel superior. And they still need to control. So, the message, like the system, must keep the narcissist separate on the basis of superiority.

Because the narcissist spends so much energy maintaining the image of superiority, he/she usually doesn't take the time to be superior

However, the narcissist cannot afford to have the light shine on his/her own life. At least, not in a judgmental sense. Because the narcissist spends so much energy maintaining the image of superiority, he/she usually doesn't take the time to be superior. In other words, if you look closely at the life of the narcissist, you won't find what the system suggests is there. The family life, the study accomplishments, the wisdom, the hard work—these are almost always lacking in the narcissistic church leader.

So, if there is no real superiority, how can the narcissist make others believe in it? First, by attaining a position that grants superiority to its holders. Second, by convincing others of their inferiority.

We have already talked about church hierarchy and the help it gives to the narcissist. Those who have lived in relationship with narcissists will understand the suggestion that he/she must make you feel inferior. The church is filled with people who already see themselves as inferior, unworthy, and unlovable. All the narcissist church leader must do is help people feel that in a way that keeps them coming back for more.

The old Greeks told the story of Sisyphus, condemned to roll the boulder up the hill, then to watch as it rolled down again. Every day he pushed with his might in some futile hope of final success. Many church members feel like this describes their spiritual lives. The preacher pushes right living, obedience, and service from the pulpit. The people work hard to fulfill the expectations and commands. Then failure brings it all down again.

Each Sunday morning, the people look forward to a word of encouragement, but it doesn't come. Even when the message is somewhat encouraging, the blessing is corrupted by a charge to do better and more. Some leave church motivated to do better. Others leave discouraged again. Most leave feeling nothing. They have become numb to the condemnation. No one leaves affirmed… except the leaders. As the congregation is pushed back down, the leaders feel lifted up. The truth is the distance between them has grown.

And, since cognitive dissonance will not allow the people to think someone could give a message calling them to something he has not accomplished himself, the congregation will believe the preacher is truly superior.

The message of the church is a message of hope. There is a better life, forgiveness for sin, and love for the heartbroken. All of this is found in Jesus. Sadly, that message is often twisted into a series of goals promised to those who try harder and find success. Those who serve enough, give enough, pray enough, and are good enough—they will find these things. And the light of hope is diminished by the reality of daily life.

The message of the narcissist, both in and out of the church, is that the people around him/her are never quite enough. If they work hard, they will almost be accepted, almost forgiven, almost loved. But being enough isn't possible. It cannot be possible, because control comes with a climate of shame and failure. There is hope, the people hear, but you must try harder.

Then comes the rub. The narcissist leader will tell you how to try harder. You can get the answers from the narcissist. He/she will guide you into truth and show you the way. The narcissist reveals your need and tells you what to do to overcome it. "Twelve Easy Steps to Righteousness!" "How to Feel Forgiven!" "Discover a Better Life!" The message always says two things: you don't have it now, but you can get it from the narcissist.

If you will forgive the wordplay, I call this the "blame, shame, and game" message. First, the leader finds something for which the person can be blamed. Any sin would be good enough, even something that might not be sinful. These are the folks who blame a group for something one member did. They assign blame by skin color, political party, or age. Victims are blamed for the actions of their abusers. Finding blame is a narcissistic hobby.

Once blame is established, and everyone can be blamed for something, then the leader attaches shame. Blame validates shame. If there is legitimate blame, the burden of shame can be placed on the shoulders of the person. Recent sins, long past sins; if there is sin, there can be shame. And shame is very valuable to the narcissist. If the person feels shame, he denigrates himself, seeing himself weakened and reduced. From that humbled place, the person seeks redemption and help.

To game someone is to manipulate them for your advantage. It usually involves some deception or trickery, but mostly it means to exploit some weakness or openness in the opponent. Players play people, we say. Narcissists weaken their opponents, then pretend to care and help. (Oh, and everyone is an opponent!)

So, the leader has the secret knowledge, the information the people need and only he knows. Now, in order to have some hope of being relieved from the burden of shame, the people must listen and affirm the leader. His position on the pedestal, over all the people, including other leaders and staff, is secure.

The "blame, shame, and game" message is not limited to the senior pastor, however. Lower level leaders can use it as well. In fact, other church members can use it with each other. Once the message is established in the church, it can be used by anyone. The shame causes people to focus on the floor in front of them, to see themselves as less than others, rather than equals.

The message is an important part of the narcissistic church. It allows the same standards to be placed on everyone. The system, politically or organizationally, may play favorites, but the message must not. The message keeps everyone under control. If the narcissist pastor, for example, needs to deal with an elder, the message will allow a basis for discipline. Higher church leaders hold lower church leaders accountable to the message, even though they might let them off if the system needs them. Everyone is accountable to the message (except, perhaps, for the preacher, but that's another chapter).

Narcissism in
the Church Culture

The Story of Julie's Friend

Julie met Marcy at the Ladies' Bible Study at church. Marcy sat in the back and stayed quiet. Several ladies spoke with her, but she brushed them off. When Julie reached out, Marcy seemed to come out of her shell. Marcy and Julie hit it off immediately. They started spending time together: shopping, having lunch, and just talking. Marcy was single, without kids, and Julie was married with two kids. Neither had jobs. At first, Julie enjoyed having a special friend. Marcy seemed to be a great listener, even a counselor of a sort. Julie found it easy to confide in her.

Julie's husband, Doug, was concerned about the amount of time Julie spent with Marcy. Julie often found it easier to get into relationships than to get out of them. Sometimes, Julie wasn't home yet when the kids returned from school. That wasn't a big problem, nor was it a problem that Julie didn't cook supper. Doug could cook and didn't mind getting something ready. But Marcy called almost every evening with something, some news or some challenge that needed Julie's help. She sat with the family in church, next to Julie, where daughter Sally used to sit.

More and more, Marcy called or came over during supper and other family times.

Finally, Julie and Doug agreed that the relationship needed to cool. She called Marcy to tell her she needed more time with her family and wanted to be there when the kids got home. She also asked if Marcy could refrain from calling in the evening. Julie felt bad asking these things but needed the time.

Marcy began to accuse Julie of abandoning her, just like others had. She said Julie was a phony friend who never really accepted her as an equal. Marcy shouted and ranted, then became quiet. Finally, she said she had to hang up.

Julie shook as she hung up the phone. Doug noticed and wondered what had happened. She told him about the call. Both thought Marcy reacted too strongly. Julie decided she would call Marcy in the morning.

But in the morning, Marcy didn't answer. Now Julie became worried. She got the kids off to school and headed over to Marcy's house. Marcy answered the door. She invited Julie in, but seemed distant or angry. When Julie asked why she didn't answer the phone, Marcy said she saw who it was and thought Julie was "just calling to yell at me some more." Julie denied yelling at her and apologized for upsetting her. She said she thought Marcy would understand she needed time with her family. Marcy just nodded her head and said she spent the evening by herself.

Julie didn't know what to do, so she made up an excuse and left. She felt like she had lost a friend.

The Ladies' Bible Study met two days later. Julie called Marcy to see if she needed a ride, but Marcy didn't answer again. When Julie arrived at the church, Marcy was already there talking and laughing with the other women. As Julie walked into the room, things grew quieter until Marcy welcomed her with a warm hug. Julie thought that strange and backed away a little in her discomfort. The others watched.

The study went well, and Marcy seemed to enjoy the fellowship afterward. In fact, she laughed and talked more than usual. She was polite, even kind, to Julie, but didn't spend much time with her. Some others talked with Julie, asking her how she was feeling lately and how Doug was doing. Julie tried to get a chance to talk with Marcy alone, but it just didn't happen.

That Sunday, at church, Marcy sat with another lady from the study. Sally got to sit by her mom again. Things were getting back to the way they were before Marcy came into Julie's life, but Julie wondered what she had done wrong. She accused herself of being unkind in her words, of not expressing herself well, and of not being a good enough friend. Doug could see she was unhappy but didn't know how to help. He enjoyed being a family again.

Later the next week, the leader of the Bible Study called Julie to see how things were going. She said she had been praying for Julie and her family, especially her marriage. Julie didn't understand. She asked why these prayers seemed necessary. The leader said sometimes she gets the idea that certain people need certain prayers. Julie thanked her.

For the next couple weeks Julie felt like the church had changed. She didn't feel as comfortable as she once had. Finally, one of her friends invited her to coffee. They talked about all kinds of things, then the friend asked what happened between Julie and Marcy. Julie told her, but then asked why. The friend said Marcy had been telling people how Julie was changing. She suspected something was seriously wrong in Julie's marriage. She said Julie told her that Doug got angry when she didn't have supper ready or wasn't there when the kids got home from school.

When Julie tried to explain what had happened and how Marcy had twisted the truth, her friend suggested she should go to apologize to Marcy. Julie said she had already tried but didn't believe she had done anything wrong. The friend said hurting Marcy's feelings was wrong and warned Julie that little sins can cause great heartaches. She reminded Julie that the church offers free marriage counseling.

Julie left the coffee shop reeling. What had happened?

Narcissistic Friends

Yes, in the story, Marcy was a "covert" narcissist. Unlike the "overt" narcissist, who may be hard to miss, the covert narcissist is often quiet. Instead of being loud and boastful, instead of seeking the limelight, Marcy gets control through being a needy person. She consumes the life and energy of others. Instead of building herself up, she pulls herself down and expects others to lift her up. When she has drained the energy from her victim, and sometimes this means many resources, she drops the person to find someone else. If the victim should realize what's happening and begin to pull away, Marcy attacks. She has listened to gather compromising information, and she isn't afraid to spread that information around to shame her victim. This is a classic story of narcissistic friendship.

In the church, another dimension is added. The narcissistic message assumes Julie is at fault. It doesn't really matter whether she did something wrong with Marcy. What matters is Julie has done things wrong in general. Julie is lacking... and it is the job of the church to show her that. The "friend" personifies the message.

When Job suffered the various tragedies of his life, he could see no cause for them in his actions or attitudes. The Scripture makes it clear to the readers that Job was not to blame for his suffering. The point was not that Job had sinned. Instead, the point was that Job would remain faithful through the trials. He did remain faithful, until his friends came to help.

Someone once said Job's friends were great until they began to speak. In fact, they were great for a whole week. They just sat there in sympathy. But, when they started to speak, the blame and shame message came out. They assumed Job had sinned, because the message they knew said we are all responsible for the trouble we experience in life. Instead of encouraging Job, they established his blame, secured his shame, and sought to game him into right behavior. If he would just publicly confess his sins and change his ways, they suggested, things would start going his way again.

When Job protested these accusations, his friends accused him of being self-righteous. He wasn't humble enough. If you study the story, it isn't until Job becomes frustrated and begins to accuse God of being unfair that he gets into trouble. I would suggest, as the friends of Humpty Dumpty said, he was pushed. The unfairness of the narcissistic message, brought to him by those he thought were his friends, was too much to bear in his grief.

Julie's friend from church brought a not-so-subtle reminder that Julie was always at fault about something. The more Julie protested, the more sin she revealed, according to the message of the church. Surely there was some way in which Julie had offended Marcy. Surely there was some unkindness, some selfishness, some lack of compassion, that caused poor Marcy to do what she did. If Julie claimed she did nothing wrong, that alone would be sin. According to the message of blame and shame, there is always something.

This is the same message that blames the abuse victim for the abuse, the rape victim for the rape, and the abandoned spouse for the abandonment. There must have been something the victim did to deserve what she/he received. The message brings judgment in the form of blame and punishment in the form of shame. We see it and abhor it in the extreme versions, but the same message runs through so many churches.

Notice that the message affects everyone involved in the church. It pervades the membership. The pastor doesn't have to visit Julie to bring the message to her, a friend from the Bible study will do it. The person who lays the blame and prescribes the shame doesn't even have to be a narcissist. When the narcissistic message is in place, everyone will do it. The people of the church will bring it to each other.

I used to tell people in the church not to go to friends for counseling. The reason, I said, was that their friends may enjoy the drama so much that they subconsciously undermine attempts to end it. But the more serious reason is that when friends don't know what to say, they repeat what they have learned. If they have learned the blame and shame message, which most have, they will bring that to the one who is hurting. The hurting person may become confused or further victimized by accepting the blame and shame.

What would happen if Julie protested the accusations of this friend too much? What if she stood up at that coffee shop and told her friend her insinuations were wrong, and she wasn't going to listen to those lies anymore? Of course, Julie would be risking the friendship. Now the friend would feel attacked and would go back to other friends to give her report. Julie would feel more uncomfortable and more ostracized. Other friends would stop inviting Julie to events. Some wouldn't speak with her at church or at the Bible study. Perhaps Julie would stop going to the Bible study. After all, it would hurt a great deal to see her former friends laughing and chatting with Marcy while they ignored Julie.

And Julie would feel betrayed. Somehow, she would think, Marcy was able to turn her friends against her. She wouldn't understand how it all happened. She would be angry and hurt. She would probably want to leave that church and not be in any hurry to join another.

A narcissistic message will create useful, but fickle, friendships

Julie might blame this on Marcy, but she would be only partly right. Marcy did use her and hurt her, but Marcy also took advantage of a system and a message that were already in place in the church. That message is why Marcy has stayed in that church. She instinctively understood the kind of friendships that were cultivated by that message. Superficial, nice, but not loyal or sensitive. A narcissistic message will create useful, but fickle, friendships.

Of course, it is natural and commendable that people should cultivate friendships in church. Some would say their closest and dearest friends have been in church relationships. Like-minded people, brought together for common purposes, will often find they have other things in common. But there are other considerations. Churches tend to be closed groups. Members are together for reasons other than friendship. There are expectations that may not exist in non-church friendships. Differences that are natural among people in communities may not be welcome in churches. Church members may be expected to endure impositions that would not be tolerated in community friendships. Conformity and unity are almost natural church expectations, but not as much in the broader community.

In other words, church friendships have more baggage than normal friendships. If you don't want to continue to get together with someone in the neighborhood, you may not have to see that person for long stretches of time. But at church you not only have to see that abusive friend, you are expected to be welcoming and congenial. You may even be expected to trust that person again. While some might suggest that these extra pressures force us to value friendships more, they would allow abuse in a narcissistic system.

As in Julie's case, the narcissistic message in the church changes a normal and enjoyable friendship into an opening for judgment and bondage. The narcissist will use church friendships because these friends are not quite as free to disagree or to decide not to participate. The church leadership may cultivate an atmosphere where friends share intimate, even confidential, information "for the sake of the testimony." Friends can quickly become critics, critics with information. Because loyalty to the church (denomination, leadership, doctrine, style, etc.) is seen as more important than loyalty to friends, those who feel the need to leave a church find they must also leave friendships behind. Some even experience the change of those friendships to anger and enmity.

Again, church friendships can be valuable and blessed. But the narcissistic message is pervasive, corrupting even simple and innocent connections.

The Story of Billy's Family

Billy's dad almost didn't make it to Billy's birth because he was leading a Bible study that night. He had told his wife to try to wait until he was done, but everything started to happen at once. He called her sister to take her to the hospital and said he would some as soon as he could. Billy's dad made it to the hospital and into the delivery room just in time. He got to hold Mom's hand as Billy was born, and he reminded his wife to breathe just as they had practiced. The only problem was that Billy's dad had never actually made it to any of the practice times. Mom's sister went with her. Mom told him about it and showed him in the living room one day.

Dad was so proud when Billy was born. He told everyone about the challenging delivery and how he was able to help his wife get through it. When the time came to give thanks in church, he even thanked the men of the Bible study for allowing him to leave early to be with his wife. Billy's dad was dedicated to the church.

Billy's dad was a hard worker. He spent late nights at work and at church. He gave talks for men about leading their families and raising their kids. He even spoke on loving their wives. But

Billy's family didn't get to see Dad much. He was an elder and sometimes even preached when the pastor was away. Billy and his sisters learned to be careful around Dad because he would get angry. He said he worked hard and didn't have time for kids who disobeyed. He spanked hard and didn't stop when Mom asked him to. Most of the time, Dad was mad at Mom. She didn't keep the meals warm for him when he finally came home. The house wasn't clean enough when Dad brought friends over. And she didn't work hard enough to make the kids behave.

Billy grew up thinking his mom and his sisters weren't as important as his dad and he were. That's what Dad said was in the Bible. Dad had a verse for everything. There were a lot of people Dad didn't like. He didn't like people who talked differently or didn't look like the people of the church. He didn't like policemen or his boss or Mom's family. He said a lot of people overstepped their rightful places, according to the Bible.

Dad knew a lot about the Bible. He would teach the kids and Mom sometimes, but usually he got frustrated when they asked questions or acted like they were sleepy. Then he would just quit and leave the house. He said he would spend his time with people who wanted to learn. Everyone felt bad when Dad became angry. They tried very hard not to ask questions or let their minds wander. Eventually, Dad was just too busy to have the family Bible times. No one really missed them when they stopped.

As Billy grew, he tried so hard to make Dad proud of him. He liked to build things, but Dad yelled at him when he made a mess in the garage. Sometimes Dad would take him to the special events at church where all the men would bring their sons. Then it seemed like Dad was proud of him, at least until they got in the car to go home. If Dad talked at all on the way home, it was to criticize Billy or the others. Billy learned how to ask questions, so Dad would focus on his dislike for the other men and their sons. That way Dad didn't focus on Billy so much.

When Billy became an older teenager, a young man, he had learned how to stay away from Dad, for the most part. He noticed his sisters were also afraid of Dad, but for different reasons. Mary really didn't want to be alone with Dad. Sometimes she cried, but never so Dad could see. Billy knew Mom cried, too.

Billy and his sisters left home as soon as they could. One of the girls was married young. Billy went to Bible college. Dad was happy about that. The other girls found jobs in other cities and moved away. That left Mom and Dad alone. Family gatherings were expected on holidays, but Dad usually spent the time lecturing the young people about the sins of the world. Judy and her husband rarely came to these gatherings. Dad wasn't happy about that but decided Judy should honor her husband's family now that she was married. When Billy graduated from Bible college, Dad thought he should come back to work at their church. He could live at home. Billy was thankful the church leaders decided it wouldn't be a good idea to hire him. He stayed in the city where he went to college and got a job at a grocery store. He called his mom when he could. He came home when he had to.

When Billy grew up, he didn't go to church very often. When he called home to talk with Mom, his dad would usually ask if he had started going to church yet. When Billy said he hadn't, Dad would say something about Billy suffering the consequences. Billy didn't argue because it never did any good to argue with Dad. Usually Mom was the one who suffered later, Billy's sisters said. Mom would say it wouldn't hurt Billy to go to church once in a while, just so he could have something to tell his Dad. Billy didn't see much value in going to church.

As Dad grew older, he seemed to become angrier. He hated almost everyone with what he called "righteous hatred." He would quote the Bible, often incorrectly, to justify his meanness. He said the people would become more and more corrupt and then God would deal with them. He stopped teaching the Bible study because no one came anymore. This was proof, he said, of how compromised the church was getting because of the new pastor.

The Narcissistic Family

Many new believers wish they had grown up in a Christian family. They look back at alcoholic or abusive parents, broken homes from divorce, cruel or manipulative friends and family members—and they think those who grew up in Christian homes had it made. In some cases, they are right. Many children of Christian families grow up knowing they are loved, even when they do something wrong. They grow up in secure and supportive homes and in church communities where right values and compassion are encouraged. But this isn't true for all of those who grow up in church-going homes.

Billy's family, we might say, was dysfunctional. But no one at church could see it. All the church members would have seen was a man dedicated to the Lord and a submissive family. Mom may have been quieter than some of the ladies, but she didn't seem to be abused. The kids were exemplary in their behavior, something the church members commented on more than once. Dad was an accomplished teacher who, many thought, should have been a pastor. What a great family!

The fact that Billy's family looked better than others was part of Dad's plan. He may not have done much as a father, but he demanded and obtained control over his family at church. If someone thought one of his kids looked unhappy, Dad would say she was sick. Then he would take her off to the side and threaten her for acting sad. He would make claims about how well his kids did in school, how well they knew the Bible, how well they behaved at home. He would even brag about Mom. At church. At home the claims became accusations. But, at church, Dad's family was very good.

Churches that teach their people to live by comparisons and standards often encourage them to become "creative" in their reports about family life. Holding up an image for the people to emulate, often (but not always) the pastor's family, moves the people to stretch toward that image. Stories are told, sermons are preached, conferences are promoted to hold up the image so the families of the church can be said to be superior to those in other churches. Superior doctrine, superior preaching, and superior families are hallmarks of many churches.

The narcissistic message does not build families. Rather, it builds the image. Remember "blame, shame, and game." Disobedience in children, friction between husband and wife, these are evidence of sin according to the message. Any family that experiences these and other negative behaviors must be doing something wrong. Members of the church are free to speculate, if the information is not given by the father or the pastor. There must be compromise somewhere. Often the father will pass the blame to his wife (as Adam passed the blame to Eve), but with a compassionate word. "She tries, but just doesn't have the skills. Her family never taught her what it means to live rightly." Blame rarely stays with the one accused because it is so easily passed on.

The narcissistic message does not build families. Rather, it builds the image

But the family that can't escape the blame will also not escape the shame. Actions or attitudes that are considered negative must be dealt with swiftly and decisively, or the shame will fall like darkness on the family. Young people who get arrested or become pregnant or act out in various ways prove blame on the parents and bring shame on the family. The narcissistic message allows this, even demands it. Shame, that humbling that moves a person toward submission, is the tool the church uses to push the negative away from the image.

No narcissistic church can have families where the children are disobedient. That doesn't fit the image. When it happens, the system assigns blame, covers with shame, and offers the game. If the family will begin the new seven-step program, perhaps led by the pastor or a chosen leader, then maybe they can recover from the shame. Not all the way, of course. The system remembers those who threaten the image. But there is hope for a family or a person—if they are willing to play the game. Public confession, public repentance, public change: these may be expected in dealing with the shame.

At home, the families under a narcissistic church message may suffer from double-mindedness. On one hand, children are children. They want to play. They get dirty. They struggle with rules and expectations. Play, dirt, and noise normalize a young family. On the other hand, parents know they could face judgment at any moment. Someone from the church could drop in. The house must be clean enough, the kids controlled enough, the activities productive enough.

The burden of the message creates a false reality. Just as the narcissist must establish and support a superior image, the narcissistic message continually expects support for the perfect family. Whatever the truth may be, the very best must be presented under that message.

For example: the children are playing and laughing upstairs, the television is on in the living room, Mom is dressed in her old jeans, and someone has left a mess on the dining room table. Suddenly the doorbell rings. Within seconds, the television set is off, the kids quiet down, and the mess from the table is gathered to a place out of sight. Mom rushes to her bedroom, telling one of the children to answer the door. She quickly changes to an acceptable skirt and comes down the stairs to greet the visitor. For all the visitor knows, the family that is presented when the door opens is just as they always are.

This duplicity is more than a simple deception. As it sends a desired message to the visitor, one that supports the image, it also sends a message to the children. They learn normal activity is not good, perhaps evil. They learn abnormal activity (what family lives like that?) is desired. When two of the children come running down the stairs, one chasing and the other screaming, Mom scolds them and sends them to their rooms. The blame is entirely on the children and so is the shame, at least that's what Mom hopes. The children learn there is no fun when visitors are around, especially church visitors.

The narcissistic message condemns everyone (blame) so everyone will become submissive and controllable (shame) and look to the narcissistic leaders for hope and direction (the game). Parents and children learn that being themselves is wrong. Their natural impulses are always evil. Their behavior and attitudes will always be expected to conform to the image.

This message fits with what narcissists learned as they grew up. They also learned they could never be themselves, that they must maintain the image. They became judgmental and dismissive of others in their need to project their superiority. The message promotes comparisons and levels of success. Narcissists know where they are in that system, and they know how to climb the ladder.

In a sense, the narcissistic message makes narcissists of all the members. Dad, in the story, certainly acts like a narcissist. He is driven to maintain the image. He shows little or no empathy. He is borderline abusive, perhaps crossing that line in his discipline and in his relationship with his daughters. He cares about nothing more than being better than others. Yet, he may not have grown up this way. He may be showing these characteristics because he has accepted, for himself, the message of blame and shame. He is now playing the game.

Mom is not a narcissist in the story, yet she deceives visitors and church members regarding her family life. She supports and enables her husband in his striving. She loves her children but contributes to their struggle with reality. Sadly, she lives the inconsistent life, under constant tension and shame.

The church organization will continue to use Billy's family as long as things don't fall apart. Dad will be expected to do even more, Mom will be expected to continue to give support, and the children will be expected to continue to fit in. No thought will be given to the cost this might have for the family, because all the other families live under the same message. If Mom were to complain to one of the other wives, she would be told to bear her cross and give thanks for her wonderful husband. She would reveal something negative about herself. If Dad found out, he would think she suggested blame for the family, particularly toward him. He would become defensive and try to turn the blame toward her. She would learn quickly to stay quiet.

If Billy's family should become compromised, they may be set aside. Dad could be asked to stop teaching the Bible study, "until he gets his house in order." They would feel the eyes of the congregation as they entered the church and may even hear their story in the pastor's message. Friends may not be as friendly. Opportunities may disappear. Dad's family image will diminish. Marginalizing is the new shunning. If possible, church leaders will help Billy's family through a special conference or training or even counseling. If they play the game, they may be restored.

Tim and Marj's Story

(Warning: this story might present triggers for those who
have been through abuse.)

Marjorie met Tim at a denominational gathering of churches.
Young people came to hear messages designed to help them find
God's will for their lives. They learned about missions and
serving in the church and what Christian marriage means. Tim
went to a church on the other side of the city, a small church
where his father was the pastor. Marj's family attended a large
conservative church, and her parents were active in the
children's ministry.

During one of the breaks, Tim started visiting with Marj.
They laughed about a story one of the speakers told. Tim said he
knew someone just like that. Marj was impressed. He was gentle
and a good listener. She told him more about herself than she
normally would, but he asked good questions and made her feel
important. Tim was a clean cut, serious young man who said he
was considering becoming a pastor like his father. They talked
through most of that break and found each other again during the
next one.

When Tim asked if they could get together that evening, Marj told him she was expected at home. Tim quietly said he understood. He seemed a little hurt, so Marj suggested they find each other during the first break the next day. From that time on, the relationship moved quickly. The two spent a great deal of time together, even though they didn't go to the same schools. When Marj graduated, Tim was there. He joked with her parents about how he helped her get through her finals that last semester. Everyone in her family got to meet him. When Tim graduated, Marj wanted to be with him, but he said he wasn't going to the ceremony. He said his parents had something at church that night, and he had to be with them. Later, Marj found out he did attend his graduation ceremony but spent the whole evening at a party with his friends.

Marj's parents cautioned her about Tim. Things were moving too fast, they said. They acted as though they didn't trust him. She defended him and felt herself drawn even more to him. He wavered between being hurt by her parents' concerns and not caring at all. Instead of going to college, Marj decided to get a certification as a dental technician. Tim encouraged her in that because he said she could get a good job right away, without spending a lot of unnecessary money. Marj's parents had always planned on her going to college but were willing to let her make the decision. She also started going to church with Tim at his father's church. She missed her friends, but liked Tim's family, for the most part.

Marj didn't get pregnant before she and Tim were married, but almost. There were some anxious days. He pushed her to be intimate quite early, but she was convinced it was because he truly loved her. He said he just wanted to be as close to her as possible. Marj felt ashamed after the first time, but then it didn't seem to matter as much. Besides, Tim said they would get married. They just had to wait until Tim got a good job. He rarely talked about becoming a pastor. When he did, he said he didn't want to go back to school for so long. Instead, he got a job at a car lot, cleaning the trade-ins. He often came back with things he found in the cars. Eventually, he moved into a sales position and did very well. People began to say Tim could sell anything to anyone.

Finally, Tim and Marj were married. Marj's parents and friends expressed their concerns, but Marj really wanted their relationship to be blessed by God. Secretly, she wondered if she was doing the right thing, but she thought it had to be right. The ceremony was simple, and everyone congratulated them. Her only wish was her parents could have been more involved than just paying for everything. But her friends stood with her, and she was happy.

Marj cried on her wedding night. She didn't have regrets, but Tim was unusually rough and demanding. He reminded her she was supposed to obey him and do whatever he asked. When he went to the shower, she thought about how different this was from what she had dreamed about. She would obey him and work to please him, that wasn't the problem. She loved him. But she didn't feel as loved by him after that night.

Nearly every day, Tim came home angry. He didn't like the people he worked with. He said they were stupid. He said he could sell twice as many cars if they would just get better trades. Marj knew Tim lied to his customers about the cars he sold. He just said he told them what they wanted to hear. She did what she could to calm him when he was angry and encourage him when he was depressed.

Her job was going very well. She got raises and better positions. Tim began to be jealous of the dentists she worked with. He said she must be leading them on to get such good treatment. He had pet names for each of them, derogatory words that rhymed with their real names or described their physical features. Marj didn't like him speaking evil of them, but when she tried to get him to stop, he almost accused her of preferring them over him. She started to be afraid of what he would do if he really thought one of the dentists was paying her special attention. At the same time, she found herself wishing someone would think of her that way.

When Tim came home from work and told Marj he had quit, she was shocked. Despite his constant complaining, she never expected he would be upset enough to quit. But she learned from a friend that Tim had been fired. There were serious accusations about him skimming accounts and taking illicit money from customers. The bosses didn't want to get the police involved and ruin Tim's career, they just wanted him out of their place. When Marj asked Tim about being fired, he pushed her onto the floor and stormed out of the house. That was the first time he hurt her. Marj cried, but knew he was just upset about the job.

They still had some savings, Marj thought, and she had a good job. They could make it until he found something else. But when she looked at the bank accounts, she learned there were no savings. Not the money they had put away from their jobs, nor the money her grandfather had left her. Marj didn't know what to do. The last time she confronted Tim, he pushed her down. What would he do this time? For the first time, Marj was afraid of the man she loved. But she didn't say anything to anyone. She just went to work and did her best, even through the morning sickness.

Yes, Tim was out of work and Marj was pregnant. That would be a recurring cycle in their marriage. He went from job to job, always making good money until something happened. But, after the first baby, Tim demanded that Marj quit her job. He said she should stay home with the baby. She cried as she told the dentists she wouldn't be working there any longer. They said she would always be welcome back, but she knew they would fill her position quickly.

Tim lived his days as an angry man and took his anger out on his wife and kids. He never hit the kids, but Marj wouldn't say what happened to her behind closed doors. She tried to talk with one of the ladies at church, but she was told that suffering was part of the job of a good Christian wife. If her husband wasn't happy, it was at least partly her fault. Then she was told not to talk to anyone else about it. She wouldn't want them to think poorly of the pastor's son. So, she kept quiet until that day.

On that day, Tim came home very late again, near one in the morning. Marj asked him what he had been doing so late, and he reached over and slapped her full across the face. Marj fell back onto the bed trying to get away from him. He glared at her and said she should never ask him that again. The next morning, he said he was sorry she had made him do that. He would try hard not to do it again if she would try not to provoke him like that.

Then he left for work. Marj was still shaking. She didn't know what to do. She thought she couldn't go to the police because the redness on her cheek was already fading. He hadn't slapped her that hard—yet.

She decided to go to the church's counselor, a man trained by the church and paid to help with marriage problems. Frank, the counselor, listened to Marj's story and said he sympathized with her. Tim certainly should not have hit her. But had she considered what she did that hurt him? He told her about turning the other cheek and submitting to her husband, the kinds of things Tim's father preached about. Then he said he would keep this confidential, but if it happened again, he would have to go to the elders. That meant Tim's dad would be involved. But he would pray for Marj and Tim. Maybe this was a fluke. Maybe Tim was just upset about his work. Sometimes men are under a lot of pressure, he said, and a good Christian wife should help to relieve some of that for her husband.

Marj left the office that day knowing both that her trouble was just beginning and that the church was not going to be a place of support and refuge.

The Narcissistic Marriage

I stopped Tim and Marj's story before the end, but it doesn't get better. I wish I could say it was all fiction, but the story is made up of true stories I have heard in my counseling and reading over the years. Some will read this and be amazed at how well it describes what they experienced. I wish that wasn't true.

Far more has been written in popular literature about narcissistic marriage relationships than other relationships. There are a few books out there about parent-child relationships, even some about work relationships. But struggles in marriage are much easier to read about than talk about. Some have only understood the stresses they face every day when they picked up a book about narcissism and marriage. Some of these books have been written by therapists and counselors; some by psychologists; some by victims. One popular book was written by a narcissist. Books on marriage sell, but books on narcissism in marriage often meet real needs.

To adequately cover the tactics and struggles of narcissistic abuse in marriage would take a hefty book. Many of the narcissist's tools are most clearly seen in marriages. Gaslighting, projection, lying, manipulation, and more are suffered by spouses every day. Even counselors who do not deal with marriages should read some of these books to learn about narcissism and narcissistic techniques.

One would hope that victims of narcissistic marriages would find help in the church. We know marriages suffer stress, not in the least from the fleshly perspectives of each partner. When two people bring their brokenness together to try to make one life, we should understand the friction and the challenges. But we should also understand, knowing the internal struggle with sin each person faces, that one person could harm or abuse another. Marriage abuse should be something the church is prepared to address.

But victims of narcissism rarely find this to be true. Women and men report feeling as abused by the church they trusted for help as by their narcissistic spouses. Like Marj, these women go to other women in the church for support and find judgment and criticism. When, and if, they go to a church counselor or pastor, they are treated as the offenders, rather than the victims. Male victims come away feeling like failures, incompetent to "handle" their wives. Men and women alike often say the church pushed them into being quiet. Many have walked away from the church for years after struggling in a narcissistic relationship.

We have already looked at why narcissists seem to be drawn to churches, especially to positions of leadership. We have already considered why the performance system creates a haven for narcissists and other abusers. These would be serious reasons why victims wouldn't find much help in churches, but beyond these there is much more. Frankly, the church is ill-prepared to meet the challenge of narcissism in marriage for some specific reasons.

First, the teaching of many churches provides support for abusers by preparing people to be victims. No, this isn't about doctrine in the usual sense. There is an underlying theology, or anthropology, most churches share that keeps victims in places of risk and pain. I would call this a theology of guilt and suffering.

> The teaching of many churches provides support for abusers by preparing people to be victims

Most church members have been taught that problems in their lives are the result of their own sin. They know there is sin in the world, but the intense focus of the church on the sin in the heart of the individual—and the guilt that stems from that sin—moves them to believe any evil that comes their way is their own fault. Some preachers teach that disease and accidents are the direct result of the sufferer's sin. Even at times of intense grief, this theology offers shame as an additional burden. When the teaching is not this specific or cruel, church members still get the message that they should be more aware of their own sin and its consequences than the sin of others.

So, when the victim of abuse (at almost all levels) comes to the church, he or she will almost automatically receive a personal evaluation of the compromises that "opened the door" to the abuse. Sometimes the cause is directly related to the effect. The rape or assault victim dressed wrongly. The young man who was beaten should not have been out at night. The victim of a car theft should not have had such an attractive car. Sometimes the cause is not so directly related. The young man who struggles with lust has a ready answer for why he is failing in school. The young woman who has an issue with a formerly close friend should look to her own struggling prayer life. Those who believe this kind of cause and effect theology become quite creative. Sin is the cause of all trouble, they say, so we must focus on the sin rather than the trouble.

The underlying message is that if the sin is dealt with appropriately, the trouble will go away. So, the young wife should not balk at becoming more submissive so her husband's anger can be eased. She should be willing to try almost anything to help him. Otherwise she is rebellious, and that's the cause of the problem. If the trouble does not go away, it is probably some other unconfessed sin. The unending loop means the abuser can continue to abuse while the victim is held in place by this theology of guilt.

But what if the abuse is so obvious, so believable, the church leaders cannot ignore it? What if the woman comes to the counselor or pastor with a black eye? Even then, the victim is often held in place by a theology of suffering. Suffering is somehow holy. Those who suffer are particularly blessed by God, according to some teachers. If your husband strikes you, women have heard, you should give praise, because you are suffering for Jesus. When the church finally acknowledges the suffering as undeserved, the victim is told to stay and trust God will use it for good. Perhaps it will be a testimony for others. Perhaps God will work some special blessing in it for the children. Who knows? Just stay.

This theology of guilt and suffering is not taught only in marriage situations. Children are told they must continue to honor abusive parents for the same reasons. Employees are told they must stay in their jobs and bless their abusive bosses for the same reasons. We are not to give up on cruel people who say they are our friends, or on family members who manipulate or abuse, for the same reasons. Maybe it is all somehow our fault; and, even if it isn't, suffering is good for the soul.

But children can move away from parents, and people change jobs and friends all the time. Marriage has a different status in the church. Marriage is supposed to be forever. Marriage is supposed to be a testimony. After all, Paul said it was a picture of Christ and the church. Marriage is sacred.

The church has struggled for centuries with the idea of divorce. Marriage is supposed to be between one man and one woman for life. To allow loopholes to that contract is to weaken the bonds of marriage, in some people's eyes. If we open the door for abuse, especially narcissistic abuse, we might find the door open for everything. Rather than allow grounds for divorce in dangerous situations, such as physical abuse, the church often resorts to that theology of guilt and suffering. And, even among those who try not to minister with that theology, victims of abuse hear a message of resignation. "Well, what can you do? You can't get a divorce." Yes, we believe you. Yes, we see your suffering. Yes, we want this to stop for you. But we still aren't free to tell you to get out.

God hates divorce. That's what He said. How could any church leader tell a member that divorce is an acceptable option?

Barbara Roberts has written a very helpful book on the Scripture's view of divorce. (Roberts, 2008) She particularly deals with that question. She suggests that spousal abuse, which would include malignant narcissism, is a breaking of the marriage covenant. In her view, the marriage is already broken when there is physical or emotional abuse or adultery. Her book is worth reading.

Sadly, this kind of closed counsel, leaves victims with no choice but to leave the church. They may find a more relaxed church, one that understands the sad need for divorce in these extreme situations, or they may leave altogether. Many have felt the church left them. When they tried to get help and support, it wasn't there. No one cared. Everyone kept trying to keep them in their place.

Narcissists recognize and use the boundaries within which others live. They don't like boundaries around them, but they exploit boundaries around others. Some women have said their husbands will do hurtful things and then remind them that disobedience or divorce is sin. When church doctrines or systems are designed to keep marriages together—no matter what—spouses feel trapped. That trap allows the narcissist to continue abusing. This is not just true for marriage. Young people, often well into the college years, are told they must obey and respect their parents regardless of abuse and manipulation. Employees are told to stay in their jobs to honor their employers. Certainly, members of churches with narcissistic leaders are expected to stay and obey. This bondage is attractive to narcissists.

The first physical abuse must be seen as a serious offense worthy of outside intervention

A caveat seems necessary whenever I say anything that might seem to lessen the sanctity or value of marriage. We believe marriage is holy and honors the plan of God for His people. We also believe marriage is meant to be a blessing and joy to them. When marriage becomes bondage or torture, which it does for some, then the church has an obligation to intervene and help. Victims should be protected and comforted. Abusers should be disciplined. If church discipline or strong admonition is not enough to stop the behavior, or if it escalates to danger for the victim, then secular authorities should be asked for help. When the abuser mocks church authority, or when church authority is either unwilling or unable to stop the abuse, those secular authorities must be called. The first physical abuse must be seen as a serious offense worthy of this outside intervention. Psychological or emotional abuse should be understood as abusive and inconsistent with anything the church represents.

Some will consider this too harsh. Others will consider it too easy. The church does have a place in helping its people live joyful and peaceful marriages. But it is not the only place with authority and interest. The state also has its place. Churches often have mandatory reporting responsibilities and should never consider their jurisdiction above that of the state when it comes to abuse.

So why don't churches do well helping people in difficult marriages? Apart from a blind obedience to the idea that marriage must never be broken for any reason, the church may simply be incapable of dealing with the intensity and intricacy of marriage problems. Pastors are usually poorly prepared for counseling. Most have received only a couple of classes to enable them to help with the wide variety of stresses their members will face. Many have been taught to distrust secular psychology or therapy. Those who believe the Bible is sufficient for every situation in life usually wield a set of proof-texts that do more to discourage and alienate both the abuser and the victim. It would appear that the church, almost across denominational lines, simply wants its members to stay in their places.

Narcissists present serious challenges for counselors at any level of training and skill. Usually very intelligent, they know how to manipulate what people think of them. I have referred to this as the "narcissists' superpower." From earliest ages, narcissists have learned to deceive and beguile others. They are adept at convincing, exploiting, and influencing. Many times, victims have told me the counselor was completely seduced by the narcissist abuser, making the victim feel both betrayed and defeated. Counselors report intense dislike for the narcissist at other times, primarily because of the continual sensation of being manipulated and controlled. As I have trained counselors, I have suggested that if they ever fantasize about murdering a client, they might be dealing with a narcissist. Believe it or not, some experienced counselors have admitted to these feelings. The counseling literature that deals with narcissism regularly warns therapists of the extreme difficulty of dealing with these clients who will lie and manipulate without conscience.

So, a pastor or lay church counselor, who may have received little training, is rarely a match for a narcissist. Those bound by a system or philosophy that discourages outside contributions are faced with fixing narcissistic relationships using weak and insufficient tools. We believe the Bible has a great deal of wisdom to guide in life's difficulties, but we also know the words of the Bible can be distorted and misused by abusers to support their position. While narcissists are drawn to churches because of the opportunities for power and prestige, they are also attracted because of the weakness of authority in those who presume to hold people accountable. If the narcissist isn't the pastor or counselor himself, he may be almost as knowledgeable about what the Bible says and how it can be applied to his situation. He will almost always be far more skilled in deception and manipulation than anyone the pastor or counselor has dealt with before.

Is there a solution to this? What should churches do to help in these abusive marriages? First, churches should take responsibility to help. They should understand, more than people outside the church, that people do hurt each other, even in the most sacred and intimate relationships. Pastors and other leaders should neither be shocked nor defeated when they learn someone in their church, no matter how trusted, could be hiding sins of this magnitude. Instead of the common denial victims experience, churches should offer a rational and understanding ear of support when a victim is finally able to tell the story.

Second, churches should link to and support a network of well-trained counselors who know how to work with narcissistic relationships. Such a vocation is possible. Again, churches should understand that narcissists are drawn to systems they can manipulate, and they should not deceive themselves into thinking the church is somehow immune to this manipulation. Because of that attraction offered to abusive people, the church should do even more to train counselors and other leaders to deal with these strong antagonists. A serious Biblical perspective is not inconsistent with learning about abusive personalities and how to protect victims.

Finally, churches should view marriage as a blessing that lasts a lifetime, rather than a bond that holds victims in place for their abusers. We do not dishonor marriage when we allow a victim to escape abuse by separating or even divorcing the offender. In fact, the case could be made that this would honor marriage even more. Again, I would encourage pastors and counselors to read Barbara Roberts' book, *Not Under Bondage*. It is a carefully written and scholarly perspective on the Scripture passages that deal with divorce and abuse in marriage. There is little doctrine presented and readers are free to disagree with what they find, but we must understand the Scripture admonitions in context.

To summarize, narcissists are drawn to churches for a variety of reasons. They will use church limitations and prohibitions against their victims. Churches must be prepared to understand narcissistic behavior and abuse. Victims should find support, comfort, and protection within the church. They expect it and are hurt when it is not there. For too many, the church became another part of the abuse.

Narcissism in

the Church Structure

The Servant Story

Dick had been a member of Sunshine Church for a few years. His wife was active, but he seemed mostly disinterested. He would attend services occasionally, when the football game wasn't early or he wasn't tired from watching the late night movie. For the most part, Dick remained an inactive part of the church's life and ministry.

When the remodeling project began, Dick seemed to come alive. He went to the pastor and said, "You know, if you get me a crew and enough money, I'll get that job done." They already had a crew and a group of leaders dedicated to the project. Funds were being raised, even while the work was in progress. When the pastor told Dick he was welcome to join the other workers, Dick hesitated. "I always wanted to serve the church in a way that fits with who I am. I'd like to help make decisions, but I'll just tag along for a while."

So, Dick joined the work crew. Soon, he became the unappointed foreman of the job. He conferred regularly with those on the committee, even attending the committee after a while. No one had invited him, but he seemed so knowledgeable and so enthusiastic that the rest of the members welcomed him. Dick spoke for the work crews.

One day someone commented to one of the workers that it must be great to have someone so helpful as Dick around. "Dick?" replied the worker. "He isn't around. He comes in the morning, then heads out to the coffee shop until we are about to break for lunch. Almost every day, he checks over what we have done and encourages us to get just a little more done before we break. Most of us ignore him, but some get caught and miss the break. When the rest of us get back from our break, Dick just says we know what to do and leaves. We might see him before the end of the day, but we might not." Then the worker lowered his voice. "Is Dick really on the leadership committee? He says he is, but none of us can understand why."

When the project was finally over, Dick stood to speak on behalf of the workers. No one asked him to speak, but he walked up to the microphone anyway. "You know, this has been a challenging project. We never knew if the money was going to be there. I had to keep on top of things the whole time. We had good workers, but I had to push to keep them excited and faithful. I was active in leadership in the church we came from, but whenever I came up with ideas for those folks to do, they

111

couldn't get them done. Well, after a lot of hard work, this project is done. We owe the workers a round of applause."

Everyone applauded the workers with heartfelt thanks, but both the workers and the leaders knew Dick was taking credit for the project. It sure sounded like it wouldn't have gotten done without him. After the project, someone asked Dick to be on the maintenance committee. Maintaining the new worship and work areas would take someone who knew how things were done, they said. But Dick refused. "Not my kind of work," he said. "I'm a guy who gets things done. Others take care of things afterward. Besides, I figure I have earned enough points for my service that I can rest a while."

The Narcissistic Church Servant

"'When I was quite a young boy,' said Uriah, 'I got to know what 'umbleness did, and I took to it. I ate 'umble pie with an appetite. I stopped at the 'umble point of my learning, and says I, "Hard hard!" When you offered to teach me Latin, I knew better. "People like to be above you," says father, "keep yourself down." I am very 'umble to the present moment, Master Copperfield, but I've got a little power!'" – Uriah Heep (From Dickens' "David Copperfield")

Humility, to Uriah Heep, was the path to power. It was the way he could cope with the world and come out ahead. Although he knew others were stronger and smarter and faster, and although he didn't really want to do any work, Uriah Heep understood that life as a humble servant would give him two things. First, it would give him power. He could manipulate and influence others by his comments and actions, without drawing attention to himself. And that was the second thing humility offered him, protection. Uriah didn't want to risk confrontation or responsibility. He wanted to be free and was willing to act humbly to maintain that freedom.

Most of the popular writing on narcissism exposes and explains the overt narcissist. Loud and arrogant, overt narcissists are usually hard to miss. They want the limelight and are willing to push, fight, lie, or steal to get it. Overt narcissists talk a lot, usually about themselves. Every indication suggests they are in love with themselves. They are the picture most people have of the narcissist.

But there's another type of narcissist who breaks this mold. In fact, you might not even recognize them as narcissists. You might think they are just manipulative, needy, or conniving. They do not want the limelight, as long as they can control those who are in it. They don't talk about themselves but expect you to sing their praises and offer your service. We call these people "covert narcissists." Their narcissism happens almost undercover.

The overt narcissist may make you think of murder, but the covert narcissist makes you think of suicide. While you are frustrated that everyone seems to allow the overt narcissist to get by with so much, you don't really understand what the covert narcissist is doing to you and others. Something is wrong, but it's hard to pin down.

Covert narcissists would rarely be called abusers, but they can push people to self-abuse. Covert narcissists are not loud and arrogant but tend to be much more manipulative and subtly cruel. They don't call people stupid or lazy, at least not to their faces; but covert narcissists will make you feel stupid or lazy and leave you wondering why. Covert narcissists are the real crazy-makers.

The overt narcissist may make you think of murder, but the covert narcissist makes you think of suicide

The church, for the most part, is still a controlled group. Few churches appreciate those who push the limits and openly seek to advance themselves. Boasting is not a Christian virtue, nor is loud criticism. Overt narcissists are certainly found among church members, particularly in leadership, but not many churches can handle more than one or two. Covert narcissists, on the other hand, fit into the church easily. Their calm and submissive demeanor opens doors that wouldn't open for loud and inconsiderate overt narcissists.

But don't misunderstand. This is just another approach to meeting the same desires. The covert narcissist still wants to be in control but does so by "helping." Sometimes these folks offer to help with projects. The only problem is they end up taking over. They work, or at least they motivate you to work harder, and they get things done. But you feel stupid in the process. When the project is done, it cost more than you had planned, and it doesn't look quite the way you wanted it to. But your "helper" assures you this will be much better. Your way just wasn't good enough. This is the mother-in-law who comes to visit with her rubber gloves and cleaning supplies. You find yourself angry and wishing she hadn't come at all, when you are supposed to be grateful. In the church, these people serve on committees and take jobs no one else will take. It will be very clear they are making a sacrifice to help you, and you will be expected to praise them and honor them. Never mind that they can't seem to stay in budget or they alienate everyone else on the committee. Never mind that the Missions Committee is now somehow responsible for setting the pastor's salary and deciding what color to paint the outside of the church.

These are the narcissists who don't seem to fit the mold. They are "nice" people, people who seem to be cooperative and helpful. Their criticisms are just helpful advice. Their manipulations are just trying to encourage you. Their generosity is just trying to make things better for everyone. You will have great difficulty holding them accountable for their abuse.

You probably won't find many covert narcissists in jail. Nor will your friends understand the problem you have with them until they experience it for themselves. They will hold leadership positions in any organization—not the top, you understand—and they will mold the organization to their own liking. But they control from the sidelines, the back pews. Compared to the overt narcissists, they are gentle and quiet. But when it comes to manipulating, the covert narcissists make the overt narcissists look like bumbling clods. Very little can be traced back to them. Whereas the overt will lie and cheat blatantly, the covert will get others to lie and cheat for her. Whereas the overt will call someone names, the covert will just make you feel like the names he is calling you in his heart. The covert will apologize to you, praise you, speak words of encouragement to you, and put herself down—all to get you to do what she wants. Covert narcissists have learned to be subtle and patient.

Covert narcissism and legalism are often two sides of the same coin in the church. (I define legalism as the idea that spirituality and acceptance are based on performance.) Some who try to hold others to high standards are confrontational and argumentative. They accuse others to their faces and speak loud words of condemnation. Legalist preachers pound on the pulpit and point fingers and shake their Bibles. Some of them are overt narcissists who use Scripture to confront and control. But there are others, who are not loud or up front, who just sigh sadly and say they will continue to pray when they think you have transgressed. They ask questions like: "Do you think that's wise?" They remember sad stories of people who did the same things you are doing, and they hope you don't end up the same way. This is not covert legalism as much as it is covert narcissism, manipulation at its best.

Coverts are the experts at gaslighting and projection. They twist your words, remember things differently, and accuse—all while smiling and pretending to be your biggest supporters. And those words of apology you wish you could hear from the overt narcissist? The covert says them with a sad and believable face. You probably won't even realize it is just as much a lie as if the overt narcissist had said them.

Now, someone may think this describes the "other side" of the narcissist they know. This is what others see as you see the overt narcissist. You experience the cruelty, while they see someone who is kind and helpful and thoughtful. Or you have seen the change, the Jekyll and Hyde phenomenon. The person who was kind and helpful and thoughtful suddenly becomes abusive; and then might just as quickly change back with apologies and penance. While this could be the sign of mental illness, it may also be the covert narcissist revealing the frustration of trying to manipulate uncooperative people.

The definition of narcissism and the motivations of the narcissist are the same whether overt or covert. The tactics are the only difference. Perhaps you could say there is a difference in style. The desire for attention is still there, but the method used to get it is different. Whereas the overt will shout to get attention, the covert will speak softly so people must listen closely to hear what he is saying. Kindergarten teachers know that speaking softly is more effective than shouting to get the attention of children, so do covert narcissists. The overt narcissist will boast and get you to agree. The covert will compliment you in such a way that you turn it back to her. The overt runs for office by being everywhere and knowing everyone and attacking opposition. The covert allows others to speak words of praise for him and successfully portrays himself as humble, but willing.

The anger that is so common for narcissists is usually seen only by those who are close to the covert. Family members may know Dad is boiling under the surface. He may be using kind and positive words in a gentle tone but is holding back the anger for the sake of his image. He doesn't want the person he is addressing to think of him as explosive. Back in the car, however, he doesn't temper himself for his family. Employees know when the boss is about to come unglued, but customers will not. In the back room, the one getting disciplined will see and hear the anger.

The church offers a wonderful place for the covert narcissist to "work." The positives we attach to church service attract them. The servant is seen as "faithful," and "good," even "worthy." Narcissists want others to think of them in that way. In their hearts, the narcissists add superlatives to the descriptions. Their desire is to be seen as "more faithful," "better," or "more worthy." If anyone gets to Heaven for superior service, it should be the narcissist. After all, no one was more important to the success of the project. *— Ha!*

The only problem is that narcissists often don't like to do real work. Oh, the covert narcissist might join the cleaning crew, but others will notice she does less work and more complaining or gossiping. Since narcissists routinely do not see others as valuable, their expectations are high and their kindness is low. *Empathy* To work with a covert narcissist is to do the work yourself. When Mother comes over with her cleaning supplies, you will discover you have spent the day cleaning to her satisfaction. As she plays with the children or talks about others in the family, she will occasionally stop and comment about how much the two of you

wow!

Holy shit! Yes!

you are accountable for every

are getting done, often mentioning what it is costing her (her arthritis, the club meeting she is missing, the need to make lunch for Dad). You are worn out by the end of the visit, but she will get most of the credit. *Thur!*

Like Dick, the covert narcissist will do more to organize and goad the workers than to help with the work. Years ago, a church I served had a landscaping project to do. It would take a lot of hours and some hard work, but there were volunteers. One volunteer came to the head of the project and said, "If you get me a tractor and a group of men, I'll get that job done." Fortunately, the leader understood the real offer. This man was going to sit on the tractor and tell the others what to do. Then he would take credit for what they got done. → *yup!*

Coverts will often volunteer to "get something done." They will take over projects that are needed, particularly projects that will be noticed. But their desire for attention may be satisfied by that action. They receive praise and gratitude for taking on the difficult project, but they don't do anything. Eventually, the project must go to someone else. The narcissist will have excuses, usually ones that make him or her look good. All that was really accomplished was an unwelcome delay.

The world is learning about narcissism. The incredible lack of empathy and the willingness to use or abuse others to fulfill personal goals is being noticed. But the covert narcissists are staying out of the spotlight. They are not seen as cruel or abusive or negative in any way. They are seen as helpful. In several ways, the covert is more powerful and capable than the overt. The covert must work much harder to get the results but can often do so undetected for years. While pastors and church members seek to serve others and work for the Kingdom, these narcissists work for themselves. They discourage good people from volunteering and working. They criticize and steal credit and set unreachable standards for others. All while sounding gracious and helpful.

When Dick took credit for the work, Jack told his wife that was the last time he would ever volunteer for working in that church. Bill and Jerry quit the project the third time Dick showed up just before lunch to try to get "another half-hour" out of them. The subtle criticisms and judgments of the covert narcissist never end in some relationships. Mom is never satisfied with her daughter-in-law's cleanliness. Even when the team hits budget, the boss points out what was done wrong. It is never enough for him, but he is always in the back office. The preacher never really has an encouraging word from the pulpit, just renewed admonitions against sin. He says God loves the people, but he insinuates that God is always disappointed.

In this environment, the disheartened people find less joy and victory in life. When all the effort is still not enough, because the narcissist continues to push and take credit, people give up. They may continue to serve, but without enthusiasm. In a family, that depression can spiral to a point of hopelessness. Covert narcissists may abuse in quieter ways than their overt counterparts, but their abuse can go deeper and last longer.

The Elder Story

Exactly two months before the annual meeting, John came to Pastor Bob's office. He brought a concern the pastor had not heard before. He said he was having trouble finding a place of service for his gifts. John was a successful business owner in the city and had attended the church only a couple of years. Yet, people sought his opinion on church issues and he was considered a strong giver.

"I just don't feel like the choir or the usher committee are enough. I am happy to help with them, of course, but it seems like I could do more."

Pastor Bob asked if John had something in mind.

"Well, I don't know," John said. "I just thought maybe my knowledge of people and organizations could be of some use around here."

"I know people respect your wisdom, John, and I know you have been very faithful here. It seems to me you might do well as an elder, but you haven't been here quite long enough."

"Oh, I don't know about being an elder. That's a very important position in the church. And I don't have as much

Scripture knowledge as some of the other men. Of course, I do study quite a bit, and I have been learning. But maybe you could be thinking about how my background and leadership abilities could be used best."

When the Nominating Committee met that evening, Pastor Bob mentioned his visit with John. Two of the members voiced strong approval of John as an elder and thought he had already proved himself in leadership. Some of the members were noticeably quiet, but John's name was the first one placed on the list.

When Nancy called John to ask him to allow his name to be placed in nomination, he said he had to pray about it first. She called him back in a week. At that point, John said he and his wife had discussed how much time and energy it would take away from his family and his business and she was encouraging him to accept. He said he would.

At the annual meeting, John was the only elected leader who asked to say "a few words". He thanked the congregation for entrusting this leadership to him, especially when he was still relatively new in the congregation and wasn't nearly as qualified as some of the other men. He spoke glowingly about Pastor Bob and added that the only reason he was willing to accept the nomination was because the pastor had "twisted his arm". He had not sought the position, he said, but was willing to make whatever sacrifice was required to "get this church going again". Those words caused a chill on Pastor Bob's back.

One of the first things John did was ask the church secretary for a copy of the church's bylaws. Then he asked the treasurer for the opportunity to "look at the books." Pastor Bob knew this was unusual but couldn't really say why. After all, a good elder should know these things. He noticed John talking with people a lot before and after church. At their elders meetings, John seemed to know something about everyone. He also seemed to know all about the church's financial situation. No one could say John was slacking as a leader.

According to the bylaws, there were three months between the election of elders and the annual financial meeting of the church. But John wanted to have as much information as possible right away. He said he had some ideas of where to cut spending. Pastor Bob had no idea what John was thinking, but he knew he had been talking with the other elders and with several men of the church.

Now, everything John did had an aura of humility. Every time he asked for information, he would remind the rest of the board he was new and was just wanting to learn. He deferred to the older men as they spoke about the way things had always been, but then reminded them of how the world was changing. He shook his head as though he was just as concerned about the new styles and thinking as the older men were. But he got his message across: things would be changing.

At the annual meeting, the chairman led the discussion on the finances, thanking the treasurer and reminding everyone that prices were going up. The church was doing well with its money, but when opportunity was given, John stood up and gave his suggestions. Without the chairman's invitation, John went up to the microphone. He talked about being in business and knowing the financial markets. He suggested it was his job to try to understand what was going to happen. He asked what would change if the leading employer in town had to cut back this year. He asked how much extra money the people had in the bank or in their budgets. Finally, he suggested the budget be frozen for the next year, that nothing would be changed from the last year's numbers. Just in case, he said. Almost immediately, one of the men in the back shouted, "So moved!" Another said, "Second!"

Pastor Bob's wife, Debbie, looked at her husband. That meant they would not get a raise this year. Everything else would be alright, but the pastor's salary was the largest part of the budget of the small church. They had done well to economize, hoping this year could be better than the last. Someone stood up and asked about the pastor's pay, whether that would be affected. John looked at the pastor and asked him directly.

"What about it, Pastor Bob? Could you and your family help us out by keeping things the same as last year?"

Pastor Bob stood up and, finding some courage from his wife's look, said, "Well, we were hoping that things would change this year. We haven't had an increase in salary other than cost of living for the last few years. The church is doing well financially, and we thought..."

John cut him off. "Well, I don't know. The pastor's salary is a large percentage of the budget. What do the rest of you think?"

People started to talk among themselves. Finally, one of the men in the back said, "Let's leave everything the same." There seemed to be agreement, and the vote was taken. The budget stayed the same.

John hadn't sat down for the vote. He had something more to say. "Now, I think we just made the only decision we could, but I also think we ought to do something to thank Pastor Bob and his family for all their work in our church. I want to suggest we give them an extra week of vacation. Maybe they can do some traveling or fix up their house or do something special."

All around there was agreement with the new idea, especially when John promised he and the other elders would cover whatever responsibilities would be needed while Pastor Bob and his family were off. The vote was taken, and the meeting was essentially over.

People came up to Pastor Bob with excitement in their eyes and smiles on their faces. They congratulated him on the extra week of vacation and teased him about fishing or having more time to plan his pulpit work. Bob looked at his wife. They were both wondering how they could afford to go anywhere without more money.

Pastor Bob resigned and went to a church out of state in the same year John was reelected as elder. John became the leader of the pastoral search committee. He said he would find someone who could do the job "as unto the Lord."

The Narcissistic Church Leader

Did you see it? Pastor Bob and the congregation were manipulated by a narcissist. Having established his foothold in the congregation by his generosity and service, John then took his investment to the bank. He knew the Nominating Committee would meet that evening, and he knew there was an elder position open. His self-effacing act was good enough to pass for humility, but not so good that it offered any real obstacle to the process.

Of course, his words to the congregation were just barely within the realm of truth. Pastor Bob had not "twisted his arm," and John had successfully sought the position without allowing his intention to show. In fact, the congregation's vote was obviously right. Had any of the other elders had such strong support from the pastor? Had any of the others been in the church such a short time before rising to leadership? Had any of the others had such strong and understanding support from their wives? The congregation was left with the idea that they had not only made a good choice; they had, in fact, made the best choice.

Other than the subtle twists of truth, John had made only one slip. His statement about getting the church "going again" betrayed both a personal agenda and his negative evaluation of previous leadership. And, yes, First Church and Pastor Bob were about to see some changes.

John's image of himself is that of a strong leader to whom all people are drawn in their pursuit of goodness and wisdom. He thinks he is doing the church a favor by assuming leadership. Does that seem a little too much? Hey, it's an image, a fantasy person. Who would make their image anything less than wonderful?

The church has not often seen itself as a place where those who desire power can be satisfied. Most people see their church as a place of service, rather than leadership. The thought of someone wanting to be a part of "bored" meetings is almost inconceivable. But the narcissist has no real agenda other than to feel important. Making changes, creating factions, influencing others—these make narcissists feel important.

One man once came to me and said he thought it was time for him to be an elder. I said there was a great deal of work to be done and another elder might be a good idea. The man said he didn't really have time to do work, he just wanted to help the current leadership in making decisions. Making decisions was leadership, in his mind.

Typically, narcissists dislike true service positions in which they have to work. They might take jobs, but will find others to do them, perhaps their wives or others they can influence. But a service position that can be a stepping stone to an authoritative position is much more attractive. A Sunday School teacher could become the Sunday School superintendent and then an elder. A worker on a service project might lead the next project. Whatever it takes to gain leadership.

Narcissists are drawn to authoritative hierarchies. If there is a structure where some positions are seen as better, more spiritual, more important, or to have more control, narcissists will want those positions.

Narcissists are drawn to authoritative hierarchies

Earlier, we considered three factors that define narcissism: a superior self-image, depersonal-ization of others, and a willingness to use others to serve the self-image. Almost all church organizations offer the narcissist an environment where these factors become easy. The superior image can come from being the head of the committee, a spiritual leader, or whatever the narcissist sees as higher than others. Depersonalization allows the narcissist to see others as something less than people, usually parts of a group. Church membership under the authority of church leaders creates an excellent group by which individuals can be depersonalized. Church leadership, even on lower levels, often allows narcissists a way to use others to make themselves look good. To stand in front of others, to make unilateral decisions, to be seen as more spiritual—these all feed the narcissist.

Although I have been using men as the illustrations for narcissistic church leadership, the opportunities are available for women as well. In some churches, women are not considered for elder positions or other positions where authority resides. However, there are usually many service positions where women can hold authority over other women or children. There are even positions where women can hold authority and superiority over men. For example, the leader of the Sunday School or Children's Ministry may be a woman in most churches, even those which would never consider a woman as an elder. That position may offer many opportunities for a woman to use both men and women subordinates to build a superior image.

The purpose of this book doesn't give us the opportunity to discuss the pros and cons of this male/female distinction in the church. But we can note how narcissists will seek positions of leadership and privilege even within restrictive systems. The same system that says men are somehow more spiritual than women may support narcissism in other ways.

In some church cultures the term, "church boss," is used to describe a person, man or woman, who has such power within the church structure that he/she controls board and congregational decisions. Often, however, this person doesn't sit on any board. Covert narcissists stay out of the limelight. They prefer to be humble and deferent. Yet, these church bosses talk with people behind the scenes, and everyone knows they must be satisfied or there will be a serious price to pay. Some pastors don't know who the church boss is until long into their ministry. They might not even realize there is such a person. But the covert narcissist can effect more change and stop more progress than the ones who stand up front.

We will talk about the ultimate church leader, the pastor, in a separate chapter, but we should notice that there are people who seek leadership in the church above the pastor. These church bosses usually are instrumental in choosing who the pastor will be and when he/she will go. The boss will control board and ministry decisions in ways the pastor will struggle to understand or manage. The boss will probably be able to control the pastor's salary and other budget issues. When we consider that this power is covert, or behind the scenes, we can see how this may be the ultimate position for a narcissist who does not want to work or to have the responsibilities of an up-front leader.

Yet, because the narcissist will find it difficult to sit under the leadership of anyone else, serving with a pastor is often very difficult. The special training of a pastor tends to put the job out of reach of others. However, the narcissist will not consider further or specific education to be enough to mark the person as special. That special training actually reduces the person in the eyes of the narcissist, who would say, "Well, if I had spent all that money on schooling, I could make people think I was special, too." To denigrate the training allows the narcissist to see himself as superior. He has a "real job."

Many church systems seem to cultivate "pastor wannabes." These are both men and women who feel the need to be up front preaching and teaching despite their non-clergy status. In some churches, these folks become worship leaders, lay preachers, or even denominational leaders. They find ways into the pulpit to show their superiority. If those opportunities are not available, some may use open prayer times or special music times to offer their own insights into Scripture, so they will appear to be spiritually higher.

Again, if there is a system that lifts some people above others, narcissists will seek to use that system for elevating themselves.

The Pastor Story

First Church needed a pastor. Pastor Olson left after many years of building a strong and influential congregation. His staff stayed with the church, and things were running well. The leaders of the church believed the congregation could become something special. They visualized a church that made a difference in the community, in the denomination, and in the world. They looked for a man who could lead them into that future.

When Pastor White met with the leaders of the church, he impressed them. He was full of ideas and enthusiasm, and he presented himself very well professionally and personally. It was easy to look past the struggles he had in his last church because that church didn't have either the potential or the staff of First Church. The denomination had to come to the former church to help work things out after Pastor White left, but that only proved the problems were not connected to Pastor White.

When First Church hired Pastor White, he was God's leader for the future of the church. He was personable in the pulpit. He looked people in the eye and spoke to them as a leader should. When he met people, he shook their hands, patted them on the back, and made them feel like he really cared. At the same time, he had a vision for the future and plans to get there.

For the first year, Pastor White used sermons he had preached at his former church. That was understandable because he had so much to do to get to know the people and the community, and to fix a variety of problems at First Church. There were more problems, "bottle-necks" and "roadblocks," than anyone realized. The leadership was sorry to see some of the older programs go, but it was necessary for progress. Yes, Pastor Olson visited people in the hospital, but now that was the job of the elders. Yes, Pastor Olson attended a variety of leadership meetings, but now those meetings were handled by the staff. Pastor White was a busy man.

It was more troubling to see faithful staff members exposed as incompetent or standing in the way of growth. When Betty was let go after fifteen years as the church secretary, most of the people understood. She did talk with people on the phone longer than necessary, and she did move more slowly than she used to. Betty was replaced by a very professional (and attractive) younger lady whose primary job seemed to be to keep people away from Pastor White. The new secretary had the authority to handle almost any question people brought for the pastor.

The youth pastor left abruptly, but that made sense. The youth group wasn't growing. Pastor White said the reason some families had left the church was because the youth program had stagnated. Other staff members left, most without saying anything about their reasons or even saying goodbye to the congregation. Several of the new staff members were people who had worked with Pastor White before.

But First Church was an exciting place to be. Denominational officials filled the pulpit and inspired the congregation. Other pastors from large churches around the country were invited to speak. Even community leaders, people Pastor White met as he spent time getting to know the ones he called the "movers and shakers," came to share with the congregation. Pastor White was always on the podium with these leaders, always treated with respect by them. First Church was moving up.

The budget problems were a little troubling. The surplus from the time between pastors was dwindling. Pastor White deserved a larger salary than Pastor Olson, of course, but the staff would have to bear some of the burden. After all, Pastor White was doing a lot of their work for them. It was always a struggle for a growing church to find staff capable of leading on their own. Even the long-term associate pastor, Todd, was causing trouble. He and Pastor White seemed to be on different sides. It became obvious to the leaders that a serious change would have to be made soon.

But it was hard for the leaders to get together with Pastor White to discuss the situation, or anything for that matter. He was always out of his office, and the new secretary covered for him. He attended a lot of out-of-town meetings, spoke at conferences, spent time at community events, and had special times for reflection and devotion by himself. Pastor White was a busy man. Everyone could see that. First Church was blessed to have him as their pastor.

Pastor White came to First Church to make a difference, and he certainly accomplished that. Many of the people left, but those who stayed believed he was the greatest blessing God ever gave the church. The core purpose of the church was no longer discussed, but that was okay because Pastor White had so many problems to deal with. The staff stood against him and some former members challenged his leadership. The supporters knew Pastor would come through this and the church would be stronger. They just had to stay with him. It was a matter of loyalty.

The last to go was the associate pastor. Todd held the church together after Pastor Olson left. There had been considerable interest in making him the senior pastor, but Todd was content with a support role. He wanted to believe a dynamic new pastor could take the church forward in significant ways. He was surprised when the church leadership called Pastor White because his style and focus were so different from that of Pastor Olson, but Todd was positive, and things went well.

Eventually, the truth began to dawn on Todd. No one was safe. The more supportive a staff member was, the more advantage Pastor White would take. Todd did the work, and Pastor White stood before the church and took the credit. Pastor White would make a mistake and blame it on Todd. As long as Todd was willing to keep his place, Pastor White was happy. But the more Todd saw how Pastor White operated, the more distance grew between them. He found himself becoming a target of criticism and more.

And the pushing began. Support in front of the congregation: "We are standing with Todd during this difficult personal time." Negative behind the scenes: "I don't think you are fitting into our new direction." Todd was supposed to quit. That way anything and everything could be blamed on him.

But Todd didn't quit. Pastor White had to work for this one. People of the church remembered how Todd had helped so much through the transition. The nature of Todd's job connected him with almost all the people in personal ways. Todd had support.

So, a familiar strategy had to be used. "We are not at liberty to discuss the nature of the problem." Whoa! What did Todd do? The innuendos and the gossip began, fed by comments from Pastor White, until much of the support for Todd was gone. No one wants to stand by someone who might have done—well, whatever it was.

Finally, after several grueling months, it was over. Todd was out. This one cost Pastor White a little, but it was worth it. For the next year, any church problems could be blamed on Todd and on the battle.

Then the clincher. On the last day of Todd's time at the church, Pastor White took him out for lunch and asked, "So are we okay?"

Pastor Narcissist continues merrily on his way as the dead bodies of his former staff line the halls of First Church. But he's okay.

The Narcissistic Pastor

Pastors, company CEO's, coaches, politicians, community leaders—these are all positions that draw narcissists. What do these positions offer a narcissist?

- A certain amount of power
- Significant prestige
- Focus on attention
- Unilateral decision making
- Autonomy
- Loyal followers
- A distinguished image
- The appearance of spiritual superiority

Any position that offers all of that will be desirable in the mind of a narcissist.

As a long-time pastor myself, I sympathize with any pastor who reads that list and wonders why he/she never found those things. Most pastors experience ministry as a grueling, thankless, and humbling job. Pastors usually have little opportunity to care for themselves and their families. What they do, they do with poor salaries, constant political challenges, and little help. But that isn't true in all churches. Nor is it what the narcissist sees. In fact, the narcissist would look at us and believe we are either unable or unwilling to take advantage of what he/she sees as obvious privileges. One pastor leaves discouraged from a church that is bound with limitations and burdened by politics. Another comes in and turns the church into a dynamic and progressive organization. All it took was a ruthless drive and a magnetic personality. Narcissists can often accomplish what others cannot—because they are willing to do what others will not. All they want in return is the list above.

If you look carefully at the story of Pastor White, you will see the truth. He is an incompetent pastor. His primary skill is self-aggrandizement. He knows how to make himself look good. He is well-connected, popular, and smooth. He just doesn't know how to put together a sermon, or a committee, or a project. Other people are supposed to do those things, so he can take the credit. That's what staff members are for. Pastor White's skill is the delivery. He will buy a sermon, if he must, but his delivery will make it his own. He will claim the work of others but make that work sound much better than the others ever could.

Perhaps a distinction should be made here. Pastor White is an incompetent pastor, but he is not an incompetent leader. He is a ruthless and uncaring leader who can accomplish what he sets out to do. The church will grow because of his personality and because he knows how to surround himself with competent people whose work makes him look good. When the church grows and does well, the narcissistic pastor will look good. The required steps to build a "successful" church will also reveal a successful leader.

Of course, for the narcissist, there is only room for one at the top. Staff members who do well are a threat to a narcissistic leader. If they become noticed for doing well, they might be able to stand against him. Even as he praises his staff, the narcissistic pastor will claim both credit and superiority. Staff added under his leadership owe him for their job but have the opportunity to ride the climb. They become evidence of his superior ability to choose the right people for the job. Staff members that remain from the previous administration, however, present a risk. Their connections with the congregation and loyalty to the status quo could work against the pastor's plans. Only staff with clear willingness to submit can be trusted. This is why so many new pastors insist on the right to unilaterally hire and fire their staff. It is also why their churches suffer frequent turnover in staff positions.

Frequent turnover in church staff is considered normal

It is difficult to overstate the ease in which the church and narcissism are connected. This style of church growth, which depersonalizes church members and elevates a secular style of leadership, is accepted in nearly every denomination. It has become the model of success for many churches today. Frequent turnover in church staff is considered normal. Thinking of members as "giving units," rather than real people with real needs, has become traditional. The narcissistic pastor who does well in building a church that serves his image is seen as a model for others. Denominations choose their own leadership from these "successful" congregations.

Small churches remain small only because they have pastors who think small, according to many. The "right" pastor can take almost any church to heights unexpected by his predecessors. Those few churches that are limited in size because of their location are rarely interesting either to narcissists or denominations. Plateaued churches in communities large enough to support growth are seen as opportunities for anyone willing to uproot congregational tradition and leadership. Cleansing the church of hindering influences, no matter how much the current members enjoy the traditions or leaders, is a challenge made for a narcissist.

Some narcissistic pastors are content in smaller churches. In fact, they remain content as the church decreases in size. Narcissists vary in their drive and vision just as the rest of us do. Some don't want to enter the competition or do the work to make the church successful in the eyes of the denomination or community. Instead, they may look toward doctrinal purity or moral style to create a church with spiritual superiority. As their churches rise higher spiritually, the pastor also rises. When he stands in the pulpit of the most spiritual or moral church in town, he sees himself as the most spiritual or moral pastor. To him, size does not matter. The only thing that matters is image.

It may seem that this characteristic would be the domain of the conservative church, one whose doctrine already sets up a system of judgment and comparison. However, the liberal or social justice church can have the same system and the same type of pastor. Whenever people in the church are judged according to a set of values set up by the church or the preacher, this system of comparisons and moral hierarchy can exist. In these churches, you would find conformity based on politics, dress, vocabulary, or issues that prompt moral outrage. The pastor, if a narcissist, will cultivate these unwritten tenets as a way to make himself look good.

The isolation many of these churches experience will be used and increased by the narcissistic pastor. The idea that their church is better than others means less association with churches in the community or in the denomination. Members may hear comparisons between this church and others, almost always suggesting the others are somehow less spiritual or moral. That isolation further supports the pastor's control and, in some cases, opens the door to more abuse. Members cannot escape to another church without at least appearing to compromise the principles valued by the controlling church. To leave the church, for some, means to leave the faith—at least as defined by the pastor or the denomination. That results in separation from friends or family who continue in the church.

Members of smaller churches naturally have more personal contact with their pastors. They would see more clearly the manipulation and abuse of the narcissist. In larger churches, contact and abuse may be, at least directly, limited to staff. But smaller churches would not provide the pastor with such insulation. So, the pastor's control is often more personal. Narcissists gather information with which to manipulate people. It is not uncommon for narcissistic pastors to mention counseling situations or family struggles from the pulpit. Few would mention counselees by name, but some give enough detail for them to know he is talking about their situation. If the pastor knows these personal, and sometimes compromising details—and shows he is willing to reveal them—it becomes very difficult to stand up to his control.

Because narcissists see people as objects for their use, they have no qualms about manipulating people in hurtful ways. Nor do they care that the members feel afraid or trapped in the church. What matters is their obedience and continued appreciation of the pastor. Those who do manage to leave the church are vilified, even though they might have family who remain in the church. Shunning of those who rebel against the pastor is expected.

Occasionally, a narcissistic pastor will overstep certain boundaries or cross certain people and will bring trouble to himself. Sometimes a strong group in the church will organize to oppose the pastor and his control. In the past few years we have begun to see more discipline of pastors who have abused staff or members with a controlling hand. But this discipline rarely happens and is even more rarely revealed to the church. Instead, the narcissist simply moves to another church. If the "superpower" of the narcissist is to control what others think of him, then a sub-power must be to know what others think of him. As opposition grows, the narcissist makes plans. Before a vote can be taken, the pastor announces his call to another congregation.

For the most part, narcissists do not physically or sexually abuse. Spousal abuse may be more common among narcissists, but most will be fulfilled simply by wielding power and controlling others. At the same time, a case could be made that almost all abusers are narcissistic. There are many pastors in churches today. Of those, an inordinate number will be narcissistic because of the attraction discussed above. Of those narcissistic pastors, some will use their position and freedom to seriously hurt others. Using people as objects opens the door for serious abuse. We hear almost regularly of pastors who commit adultery with someone in the church. Some have stolen church funds. Others have abused children. When legal boundaries are crossed, denominational authorities may try to distance themselves from the pastor. Unfortunately, the new trend is to find a way to quickly rehabilitate the pastor to return him to ministry. Laypeople often wonder how this is possible, even though the church's message is one of forgiveness and restoration. But how can a pastor so easily be brought back into the church leadership? Denominational officials will argue it is wrong to allow the gifts and training of the pastor to be lost to the church. They will remind church members that we all continue to sin and the act of restoration simply illustrates the verbal message. In other words, if we talk about forgiveness, shouldn't we be forgiving?

Some are tempted to think that the reasons for light punishments and quick restoration could be of a more fleshly nature. If it is true the pastor is a narcissist, then he may well have information about denominational officials that could bring compromise. The "good old boy" system wants nothing less than exposure. Those who have compromises in their own lives may wish to reduce the consequences to one of their own just in case the trouble comes their way sometime. And, contrary to popular expectations, narcissists can be very apologetic and repentant when necessary. They know what to say and to whom they should say it. It doesn't take much to convince those who want to be convinced that a person regrets sin and wishes to make life changes.

A narcissistic system allows for multiple narcissists. Although narcissists do not appreciate lateral and direct competition, they are attracted both to systems established by others and to narcissistic leaders who appear to promise opportunities. They also allow other narcissists beneath them, as long as they keep their place. So, churches, even small ones, might have narcissistic leaders as well as a narcissistic pastor. A denomination, which is fundamentally a political organization, may also have multiple narcissistic leaders. While each strives for attention and privilege, there may be enough to go around. When one of their own is compromised the rest must decide whether to sacrifice him to make themselves look good or to restore him to make themselves look good.

The SMF Story

When the churches of Scripture Missionary Fellowship came together for their first meeting, with the express purpose of associating themselves in an organization, no one had to wonder who their first president would be. Rev. Wilbur Hoyt had planted several of the churches during his long tenure in the region. The first church planted was in Summitville. When the congregation was able to support itself, Pastor Hoyt brought in a young pastor and moved on to the next community. In thirty years, he had planted fifteen churches. After a while, others went out to the small communities in the area and planted more churches. At this first meeting, thirty-five churches gathered to praise God and pray for each other. They chose their name to reflect their work.

Twenty years later, the gathering had grown to over a hundred churches. Rev. Hoyt had passed on and the organization began to refer to itself as an "association," making a distinction between that and a denomination. Men who had shown a dedication to the Lord and to the mission principles became official leaders. Yearly gatherings did little business but served as a time of encouragement and celebration.

Seventy years after that first meeting, SMF officially accepted the label of a denomination, but still stressed the unity and camaraderie enjoyed by a group serving the Lord with a shared purpose. Men and women worked in the new denominational headquarters building. Most of the people in the more than five hundred churches still honored the traditions and thinking of the past. Some still remembered the early years.

Church planting still defined SMF, but in the seventy-second year one of the churches hit a thousand in attendance. Other than special holidays or celebrations, no church had reached that milestone as a regular event. Freedom Church in Mt. Gilead became the star fellowship everyone talked about at the annual meeting. The pastor was given an hour to share how they had accomplished the feat and answer questions from other pastors and church leaders. By all indications, Freedom Church would continue to grow. Pastor Jerry Carn enjoyed the limelight.

At the seventy-fifth anniversary, some of the oldest pastors and church leaders still remembered Rev. Hoyt and spoke of his dedication to the mission of SMF. The gathering celebrated other leaders who had planted some of the founding churches as well. The style of the meeting and celebration focused on the history of the denomination. But the new president, Jerry Carn, spoke about the future. He praised those who had gone before, but "praised in advance" those who would work to bring about a new day for the denomination. He called young men and women to dedicate themselves to the values of SMF, as outlined in the new mission statement.

Over the years, SMF enjoyed a reputation outside the denomination as a strong and faithful group. The occasional scandal involving a pastor or an association representative was quickly handled by a closed group of spiritual leaders. Fallen leaders left their churches and, for the most part, ministry in general. Some were able to stay and find work within the system. Occasionally, someone would refer to the "good old boy" network, but few thought of it that way. Most understood that a family like SMF had to take care of its own troubles.

Today, SMF is still growing. It has its own seminary, mission agency, regional leaders, and a new headquarters building. Denominational staff are chosen for their skills and are no longer expected to attend an SMF church. Paid leadership positions are sought by pastors and church leaders. Even unpaid positions look good on pastoral resumes. Denominational leaders travel around the world to share the mission and encourage the churches and missionaries. Denominational salaries are far above those of average pastors in the SMF, but most people understand that to be appropriate.

Several churches count a thousand in regular attendance, some even two and three thousand. At the same time, the majority are under a hundred people. Pastors of small churches rarely achieve denominational positions unless they are somehow connected to leaders already in place. Small churches gather for regional meetings to hear pastors from the large churches or denominational representatives speak. Keynoters at the annual national SMF gatherings include writers, television personalities, and broader church superstars. At the last meeting, the motto was, "The SMF star continues to shine brighter!"

Scandals happen more often now, as would be expected with more churches. An official process carries the offender through discipline. Some are pushed out of ministry. Others, deemed useful to the denomination, go through a "restoration" track and are restored to either church or denominational work. Critics suggest it depends on "who you know." Even churches can be disciplined in the SMF, something consistent with the group's image. The committee installs "restorative" pastors to help sort through the problems and bring the church to a better future. Some receive the suggestion that they should find another association. Critics suggest it depends on how well the church has contributed to the denomination over the years.

The number of critics grows steadily in SMF as pastors and church leaders feel less valued. The denomination no longer seems to care about smaller congregations or "less significant" pastors, they say. The good old boy system has become a narcissistic organization.

The Childheart Story

"It was a beautiful spring day in May of 1979, the 24th, at about two in the afternoon. I was driving from my hometown to the large city nearby to deliver a load of newspapers for distribution from the post office. I had a dead-end job with the small-town newspaper, and I was usually discouraged. That day, as I drove, I asked God to use me in whatever work He wanted. I just wanted to do something for Him. I didn't care what it was. Little did I know what He had in store for me." Frank paused to let everyone chuckle. They had all heard the story before, some many times, but it was tradition for Frank to tell it at the fundraising dinners.

"Suddenly, I felt a voice. I can't say that I heard it, but I sure felt it. Just deep in my heart I heard God say, 'Turn the hearts of the children to the fathers.' Well, it was so strong I had to pull over to the side of the road. I was overwhelmed with both joy and fear. The reason for the joy was obvious. I had heard from God! But I also was afraid because I had no idea what that meant. I didn't even know at the time it was a quote right out of the Bible.

"I finished my delivery that day and went home. I started to think and pray, then I started to study my Bible. I don't know how long I read that night, but I woke up a new man. I had a mission. I was going to turn the hearts of the children back to their fathers!" Frank's story continued with his own return to his father and how his father died shortly after. Then, Frank worked in the church as a youth leader, while still working at the newspaper. The youth group grew, but different from most. Frank's group included the fathers. Teenagers and their fathers came together to study the Bible and enjoy activities. Soon, he started working with other churches. The ministry grew until *Childheart* was known around the nation.

Everyone understood *Childheart* was Frank's ministry. God gave it to him. He had even written a book about it. Frank chose the board members, primarily to fulfill the state's requirement for board oversight of the non-profit organization. The ministry was affirmed by several denominations and used in many churches. Somewhere around 80,000 families had participated in the youth groups. Frank would be able to quote the exact number. He knew every facet of the work.

Frank loved being up in front of these dinners. He loved the applause and the accolades. He especially loved the testimonies that came from fathers and their children. Who wouldn't? It gave

Frank a sense of accomplishment and value. He had poured himself into this ministry, and it affirmed him.

There were struggles along the way. Frank's first wife left with his two children early on. Mona had a good job in a law office and supported the family as Frank built *Childheart*. He grew more and more distant from the family, especially as he set up his office in the city, rather than the small town where he lived. As funds came in, Frank even rented a small apartment, so he didn't have to travel back and forth every day. He did come home for most weekends. When Mona had work-related business in the city one day, she decided to stop in to see how Frank was doing. The office was locked up. That didn't surprise her, since it was lunch time. But when she went to Frank's apartment and found him with his new secretary, everything changed. Frank fired the secretary immediately, but Mona filed for divorce. He rarely saw her or the children after that.

Very few people involved with the ministry knew anything about Mona or Frank's children with her. Instead, they knew Frank's wife of nearly 25 years, Judy. They knew Frank and Judy's son, Eli, named after the prophet Elijah who had the job of turning the hearts of the children to the fathers according to Malachi 4:6 and Frank. Eli was a handsome young man who was seen often around the offices of the ministry.

Frank developed a system of lieutenants to represent *Childheart* around the country. Each state had a lieutenant and an accompanying staff with offices. Donations to the ministry were significant, but each state office had to survive on the money they raised. Any income from the ministry itself— seminars, camps, and training materials—would feed back to the national office headed by Frank. Frank had a large, but not exorbitant, salary and enough staff to keep things going without his effort. He spent most of his time traveling, connecting with influential church and community leaders, and raising money. Others wrote the materials and led the seminars, except for Frank's traditional greeting at large state gatherings.

The organization seemed to run well. Frank liked military terminology. His "generals," or board members were influential people who gathered a few times each year to affirm Frank and listen to progress in the ministry. There were plenty of men to choose from to be lieutenants in the various states. From time to time, Frank would oversee the repositioning of lieutenants from one state to another, based on their effectiveness in raising money and keeping the organization running smoothly. That led to competition among the men, but Frank thought some competition was good for them. Sometimes one or more of these men would stand at the podium with Frank. He even invited a few to teach at the national level.

If you looked at the ministry from the outside, you would notice the almost uniform positivity of the staff around the nation. The materials were glossy and colorful, which contributed to their high cost. Frank and the lieutenants told the families quality was expensive, but worthwhile. Occasionally, people on the outside would comment that the lieutenants all seemed to look like and talk like Frank. That didn't seem to bother Frank, who often said these men were like clones of himself. They were doing the work he did for years, he said. A great deal of emphasis was on how people dressed and acted in public. Frank said they had to present themselves well to show the superiority of their ministry.

If you looked at the ministry from the inside, you might see something different. Although everyone put on bright and happy faces, many were depressed, and some were angry. Everything in the ministry was built on a system of comparison. Frank's youth groups were better than others. Those in the groups were better than others in the churches. Within the ministry, some were performing better than others. Yet, the standards of comparison were not stable. If Frank or one of the other high leaders spoke on a topic, say watching television or playing sports, people in the ministry immediately began to look for compromise among their members. It was already understood that those outside the group didn't measure up, but those inside had to be examined as well. When a new product came out, even a household appliance, the members waited to see what others would do before they made their decisions. Then, everything might change based on what the leadership thought. Pressure in the group was always high.

Because the leadership positions offered superior status, men of the ministry competed among themselves to be more spiritual or conforming. If one man wanted to become a lieutenant, he might watch the current leader carefully. Positioning himself as a faithful servant to the leader, he would be ready if any change was made. In some cases, information became known that disqualified the current lieutenant, and the second was ready. With a military-like hierarchy, men and their families moved frequently, both up and down the ladder. Wives and children were carefully controlled so they didn't hinder the father's progress. Each time one of the leaders passed away, left the ministry, or was shifted to a different position, his successor was a matter of gossip and mystery. No one knew who would be honored or dishonored next.

The newcomer to the ministry, a father who brought his teenagers to his local *Childheart* group, would know nothing of this. Nor would he suspect it. He would see unity and conformity and friendliness. But in a few weeks, someone might talk with him about his son's haircut or the amount of time they spent watching football. This would first have come through the lessons, of course, but the push to conform, to measure up, would start early. So would the pressure.

The Organization

Narcissism as a characteristic of an organization is rarely discussed. Most of the popular and professional literature is about narcissistic people and relationships. Yet, the "toxic organization" often exhibits similar behaviors and values we see in individuals we call narcissists. When an organization portrays itself as better than others, morally or spiritually, and draws people to itself on that basis, it has at least one value that fits the pattern. If you consider the nine criteria to determine narcissism in Chapter 3, you can easily apply the same to an organization.

1. An organization can see itself as superior and more important than others.

2. An organization can promise its members success, status, or ideal lives, creating a fantasy based on association with the organization.

3. An organization can create an elitist system whereby outsiders are separated by jargon or style.

4. An organization can create an aura of superiority where materials, membership, and marketing all feed that aura.

5. An organization can cultivate an expectation of special treatment among its members, based on their association.

6. An organization can exploit its members and others to advance its own future.

7. An organization can both welcome and discard its members based on usefulness to the group.

8. An organization can create animosity between its members and members of other groups.

9. An organization can project such exclusivity that outsiders find themselves both attracted and repulsed.

In short, an organization can create and support an image very much like the self-image narcissists create. Now, the argument could (and perhaps should) be made that organizations are not moral entities. Only as they represent groups of individuals can they be said to have morals or psyches. In fact, narcissistic organizations can only be made that way by the people who influence them. Perhaps the founders or significant leaders brought certain values and behaviors that were narcissistic because they were narcissistic in themselves.

This can easily be granted, but it changes nothing. As the organization stands, it operates with a system that is narcissistic. Think of the three characteristics we considered earlier:

1. The superior image

2. Depersonalization of others

3. Use and abuse of others to serve the image

These three constitute the plane of narcissism, at least in practice. Where (and in whom) these exist, we have a reasonable cause for suspecting narcissistic abuse. And someone might also object that the nine criteria above are marketing strategies used by many companies and organizations. The three behaviors are simply business. And, again, there is no disagreement. Above all else, the narcissist is a marketer. He/she markets an image of self for others to buy. And every relationship is a business relationship for the narcissist. Even spouses serve a purpose and can be discarded when that purpose is no longer served. So, companies and organizations that do the same things could be referred to as narcissistic.

The church operates on four levels. Jesus had one Church in mind when He addressed His followers: those who would

166

associate with Him and with each other. That Church, of course, exists across the world and time. When Paul wrote to the churches, he revealed another level, what we call the local church. Individual gatherings of believers in specific locations. Not much later in history, another level was added as individual churches associated with others of like values. Those associations became separated from one another into sectarian divisions "denominated" by their different histories, doctrines, or styles. For the most part, denominations are political organizations designed to resource and guide (some might say restrict) local churches. The fourth level of church expression has been called "para-church," suggesting organizations that exist within or alongside local churches and denominations. These ministries usually focus on a particular aspect of the Christian life that is not being serviced by the local church or which can be serviced across denominational borders.

Few would think that the Church of Jesus Christ, the body of His people, could be narcissistic. We are called to love one another as He loved us. To sacrifice and share and work together is hardly a definition of narcissism. However, some would suggest that we do not see the Church as Jesus sees it. We only see the local church and denominations and ministries. So, our experience of the church is as open to narcissistic abuse as any other organization. We might hope to enjoy the character of

167

Jesus but we often experience something quite different. What we see is the opportunity for control, exploitation, and perceived superiority that are so attractive to the narcissist.

Our culture has a mixed perspective on narcissism in organizations. We applaud the success and growth we see in a company and abhor the abuse of employees that makes that growth possible. We see the large organization dispose of thousands of workers without remorse and little compensation, and we think disloyalty is contemptable, but we watch our investment in that same company to make sure these decisions increase our profits. In these companies we see the

Basically, we hate narcissism, but we like what it can do for us

brutality of narcissistic depersonalization on a large scale. Basically, we hate narcissism, but we like what it can do for us.

The values of business, to create income for stockholders by selling products or services, allow us to expect and even accept the pain of employees and lower managers as "just part of doing business." We understand that low-producing employees, stores, divisions, or branches should be sacrificed for the balance of the budget. We may not like it, especially when it touches us, but we understand it. When Mr. Jones at the shoe shop hired Bob Brown as his apprentice, and the increase in expense was not offset by an increase in income, everyone understood why he had to let Bob go. Everyone, except perhaps Bob and his family. Business is designed to be impersonal, even uncaring. That idea is well accepted in our culture.

But the church doesn't operate that way, we think. The church has different values. The church would never "let Bob go." Or would it?

When the church rewards its leaders in the same way and according to the same values as businesses, narcissistic abuse may well be the result. I remember a pastor who came to an older church with the call to help the church grow. Most of the congregation were older and had long relationships with the church. The pastor warned the leaders that growth would be unsettling and costly. They wanted growth. The pastor knew his career would be rewarded and admired by the denomination if the church grew. From both parties he heard convincing assurances that he should do "what it takes" to make the church grow. When he proceeded to sell the church building, with the approval of the leaders, and purchase land several miles away from most of the older members, people were shocked. When he changed the worship style from what they always had and enjoyed, people felt disenfranchised. When he didn't bother to try to appease the feelings of the older members because new members were joining rapidly, no one cared except the older members. And, when the church grew to one of the largest in the denomination, the pastor was praised and honored.

But that wasn't the only effect. When the members began to see what values were rewarded in the church, some of them began to apply those values in other ways. The process of choosing leaders changed. The staff, under the direction of the pastor, made the practical decisions. What used to be the church board became little more than a group of supporters for the pastor. Staff was hired and fired according to their usefulness and loyalty to the pastor. That expectation of consistent loyalty to the pastor's self-image permeated the church organization. Lower leaders began wearing clothes and affecting a style that expected admiration. Control and abuse became part of the normal operating procedure in the church. From the Sunday School to the Elders Board, vying for attention and position was the new game. And the church was growing so fast that no one cared who was hurt to the point of leaving.

It may be this church was not a narcissistic organization prior to the administration of this pastor, but it certainly became one while he was there and remained one afterward. Those members who were lost because of the move and the changes were not mourned. They were sacrifices for the sake of progress and growth. If they complained, they received the proverbial pat on the head and kick in the pants. Staff members endured short tenures, but left having served in the fastest growing church of the denomination. The short stay didn't look as bad on their resumes as the name of the church looked good. The new building was built at great cost and enormous debt, but people believed growth would cover it, and the facility was cutting edge. Even when the pastor left under a cloud of discipline, the church continued to grow. A new pastor was found quickly, one who would support and build the desired image. There were normal style changes between pastors, but the perspective of the church toward members and staff remained the same. Leaders made sure the image didn't suffer.

Businesses, support and non-profit organizations, government entities, and churches are all designed to manage and resource people. When any organization no longer cares about its members or staff as individuals but sees them only as tools for serving the image of the organization, narcissistic abuse happens. A small restaurant can have a narcissistic view toward employees and customers. A local children's club can use parents and staff, and even the children, just to make the club seem special. A military organization or government agency can lose sight of its purpose and become self-sustaining and abusive. And, sadly, a church can use members and staff to further image goals without concern for personal need or harm.

Perhaps we could say an organization is not an organism, but it is organic. Infections carried by its members, the organisms that live and function within it, can be transferred to the organization. One leader might bring the infection, which quickly spreads to others and attracts more infected carriers from the outside. Then, even if the original leader leaves, the infection continues. Even if many of the early members leave, the infection continues in the organization. The organic nature of the group draws its life—and its infection—from the members.

How do we fix this?

Solutions

"Don't bring me problems, bring me solutions."

This book has been written to reveal a problem. However you want to define narcissism, either by popular or clinical definition, it has come to the church. Narcissists use the church's system of hierarchy, comparison, and separation to make themselves feel good and to aid in using others for that purpose. Narcissism is a part of our culture, and it is a part of the church.

The quote above is often used to keep people from raising concerns. Perhaps that philosophy works to some limited extent in business management, but in real life it is entirely appropriate to point out errors and dangers even without providing solutions. Sometimes the solutions come from a different source than that which exposes the problem. At the same time, the solution for narcissistic abuse in the church isn't really that hard to find. Since I have spent so much time pointing out the problem, let me at least try to offer steps toward a solution. If these three simple(!) steps are followed, the narcissist would not be attracted to the church, nor would those who are already here want to stay.

Be the Church

As long as I have been in ministry, people have said the church is a business and should act like one. Almost always, that is a reference to financial record-keeping and management, but it is also a general reference to the mindset needed to make the church grow. For some, there is a mandate to grow the church, even the local church, and nearly any method that works is acceptable.

But we do not worship numbers, nor do we promote the gospel of pragmatic success. We are the Church, even at the denominational and local levels. We represent our Lord, His mind and His heart. We operate in His strength and for His purpose. This alone separates us from narcissistic values. We have no competition with secular organizations or businesses and certainly no reason to compete with each other.

The communion of the Church offers a fundamental distinction from narcissistic competition. We are one. When one prospers, we all prosper. When one suffers, we all suffer. This is what the communion of the Church is about. We are together in the Body of Christ, and not one of us is better than another. There will be no positioning when there is no power or prestige. When

175

there is no need to shine above others, there is no limelight to grasp. Our goal is to magnify the name of Jesus, rather than our own.

The pastor and members of a small church are just as valuable as the pastor and members of a large church. The custodians and children's leaders are just as important as the pastor and elders. None of us has a higher place. None of us deserves greater privilege. When we accept Christ's call to serve each other in the unity of the Church, we give up the self-aggrandizement of the flesh and the world.

In the most practical sense, denominations should stop rewarding numerical growth with political power and personal acclamation. It is easy to show and well accepted that most church growth consists of those who move from one church to another. To celebrate new believers (with the angels, by the way) is certainly appropriate, but simply celebrating numbers encourages narcissistic manipulation. Businesses focused on stock price increases may be excused for treating employees poorly, I suppose; but the church has no excuse for disenfranchising some members in order to gain others or for mistreating staff for the purpose of denominational accolades. Our goals and our values are different from that of businesses.

Certainly, large churches have a place. They can offer more entry points for seekers and more connections for members. Nothing here should be construed to suggest that small churches are better. In fact, that's the point. Local churches ought to be local manifestations of the same values and goals held by the Church throughout the world and throughout time—the values and goals of our Lord.

If anything, the presence of narcissism is an indictment the church should take seriously. Are our practices consistent with Biblical values? Do we reward appropriately those who act and live in accordance with those values? Or are we trying to beat the world at its own game, using its methods and systems to build respect within the world's system?

Believe the Victims

The subsequent abuse victims of narcissists find in the church so often comes in the form of disbelief. For some reason, we are shocked when our leaders fail. The easy response is disbelief. We blame the victim, rather than believe. The fired staff member must have done something wrong. The victim of sexual abuse must have brought it on herself. The pastor abused by the church boss must not have been a strong leader. The church member who feels like a failure must be under the pressure of some sin. Too often the church has stood alongside abusers to lift them up as innocent.

The church should understand the power of sin. We are the ones entrusted with the message of what John Flavel called "the depth of the evil of sin." We know the pain sin causes and the pull sin has on the human heart. We know how sin permeates the hearts and minds of all people and how difficult it is even for believers to stand apart from sin's influence. We proclaim the cost our Lord suffered to overcome the effect and the power of sin.

So, when a victim comes to the church for help, why would we doubt her/his word? Yes, we should investigate, but we should not doubt the possibility. Some victims have been dismissed out of hand, while their abusers go on to abuse others. In the church! If we have created a system that protects or even sanctions sin, we should repent.

Too often the church has stood alongside abusers to lift them up as innocent

178

The power of the narcissist to deceive should not surprise us. The ability of the narcissist to twist truth so the offense attaches to the victim, rather than himself, should be something we look for. We should expect that people under accusation will lie, because that's a normal and known response of the flesh. We should understand that even people of our church, people we respect and care about, could do gross evil.

The "BTK" serial murderer was a respected leader in his local church. A trusted evangelical leader was a frequent visitor of a gay massage parlor. A national religious leader has been accused of sexual impropriety by more than fifty young women. Celibate priests have been convicted of child rape. Why would any local group of church members believe their pastor or elder or favorite teacher would be above such accusations?

Because we know and understand sin, the church should be leading the culture in seriously investigating accusations. When a woman comes to the pastor to ask for help with her abusive husband, she should be taken seriously. Covering up sin is never profitable, except within narcissistic organizations. There is no reason for a church to try to cover sin. Perhaps we need to remind ourselves that the world already accepts that are often compromised, that our image is tainted.

In fact, we should take active steps to help leaders and others in the church avoid sinful situations. We know the struggle. Teachers who build large ministries should be held more accountable, rather than less, simply because we know the temptations that go along with prestige and power. Pastors with personal secretaries, leaders with access to money, denominational executives who travel without their spouses—we should find ways to protect them and our testimony.

Of course, blaming the accused is no better than doubting the victim. We know some make accusations for their own purposes, regardless of truth. We know some are willing to let others lose their jobs and reputations for personal gain. This is also something we should remember. Simple processes of investigation, counseling, and supporting can be put in place to help on both levels.

> **The opportunity to commit shameful acts does not diminish as a person rises in the esteem of his or her followers**

I remember a conversation with a friend many years ago where she claimed a priest could never do evil because he administered the sacraments. Evangelicals and other protestants would scoff at that assertion—and then make the same kind of claims about their own leaders. The opportunity to commit shameful acts does not diminish as a person rises in the esteem of his or her followers. Narcissists and other abusers will cultivate reputations and seek positions where they can practice their evil without fear of incrimination. The church, both local and denominational, should model prevention and active intervention.

Love One Another

The greatest commandment, the one that contained and explained all the others, was given to us by Jesus.

> *"'You shall love the LORD your God with all your heart, with all your soul, and with all your mind.' This is the first and great commandment. And the second is like it: 'You shall love your neighbor as yourself.'*
> *Matthew 22:37-39*

Love God first and love others. Love God more than you love yourself. Love others as much as you love yourself. If there was ever a prescription to counter narcissism, that must be it. What if the church just did what Jesus said?

Striving for position, making comparisons, grasping for attention and accolades—these are not things loving people do. Sacrifice, patience, forgiveness, compassion, kindness—these are supposed to be characteristics of Christ's people. If this was what the church was about, there would be nothing to attract the narcissist. With no limelight and no pedestal, there is no need to contend with each other.

In a context of love, the way Jesus taught, victims would find support and help. So would abusers. Offenders of all kinds would find their sin uncovered and real help available. In the church, when sin is exposed, broken people can find ways to change and support along the way. Victims would be loved and valued, and abusers, who were likely once victims themselves, would know the life-changing love that is available to them. No one would be forced to remain in an abusive relationship, and no one would be pushed aside in shame.

If we loved each other, we would not be afraid or incompetent to meet each other at the point of need. We would find ways to minister to the real needs of both victims and abusers. I remember hearing E. V. Hill many years ago as he talked about his church in the Watts district of Los Angeles. He told how a woman came to a men's gathering in the hope of selling herself. She didn't even understand what a church gathering was about. Very quickly, she was gathered up by a loving woman who told her about Jesus and how He loved her. Finding herself surrounded by the "prostitute committee" and enjoying their love and support, the woman expressed her concern that her pimp would be angry. Hill said a member of the "pimp committee" contacted the man and shared the love of Jesus with him. Both found freedom and love that night because the Mount Zion Missionary Baptist Church was ready with love.

The popular definition of narcissism points to self-love. We are told the narcissist loves himself too much to care about anyone else. In truth, the narcissist does not love himself as much as he/she wants the rest of us to love the image of self that is presented. That image is designed to keep the narcissist out of reach of our criticism or rejection. The narcissist longs to be loved but has never known love. As an adult, the narcissist stays insulated from real love.

A church that lives in and offers the love of Jesus to others consistently will be immune from narcissism. That is stated strongly because I believe that strongly. There is no attraction for narcissistic manipulation in such a church. Those who would try would find themselves so out of sync with the style and system of the church that they would have to change to stay.

Very few narcissists would stay, but maybe those who did would find the love they always desired.

Is it possible?

So, can a church truly be immune from narcissism? Could a system be designed to preclude striving for power and prestige? Could a church be so focused on the Lord and His love that narcissists would find themselves challenged and unable to manipulate or deceive? I believe the answer is yes. But, perhaps, the world has yet to see such a church.

The apostle Paul wrote his letters to the churches only a few decades after the resurrection of Jesus. Paul was an adult when Jesus went to the cross, and his ministry only lasted about 25 years. But he wrote about some who tried to use the Spirit's power to give themselves prestige and others who sought power in leadership. He wrote about those who used and abused, who pulled together factions by twisting truth to serve their own purposes. Within just a few years, narcissistic people saw the church as an opportunity to feed their desires.

It may seem inevitable for the local church and denominations to struggle against narcissism. Perhaps that's more reason for us to be diligently active in creating systems and styles that fight against it. If it has always been here, we at least should learn to expect it. We should learn to see it and know how to handle it when it appears.

Perception Management

In a theological sense, legalism is a return to the ancient Law of Moses. In a more popular sense, the word refers to the attempt to become holy or righteous on the basis of behavior or performance. In this popular usage, the link between legalism and narcissism (the narcissistic message) should be obvious. If people learn that God accepts them only because of their adequate performance, they learn to worship an image of perfection. They also strive toward that perfection in their own lives. Some teachers believe this is the appropriate teaching to help people live the way they should.

However, the unseen God, who knows all things, is far more difficult to impress than His followers. If the secret thoughts are known, and the secret acts viewed in the light, who could ever hope to please Him? This legalistic message gives no hope of pleasing God. For some, the only hope offered is that He will weigh our good works against our evil actions and save us. Others teach we are so evil that our only hope was the sacrifice of Jesus to appease the wrath of God. Even then, we are told we must sufficiently honor that sacrifice by our commensurate good works so God is not disappointed in His own kindness. Still others teach that God doesn't care about our behavior, that He resigns Himself to the evil we live, but accepts us into Heaven anyway.

No part of this message will present a loving relationship with One who truly cares about our lives and walks with us. A message of relationship, other than that of a tolerant or judgmental deity with his subjects, would be confusing to those under a narcissistic message. If parents don't connect with their children through empathic relationship, how could we imagine God connecting with us that way? Those who grow up referring to God as "Father," will necessarily think of His fatherhood by the definition of the earthly fatherhood they experienced. For those who knew only a distant, unfeeling, or cruel father, that will be their image of God.

The message of blame, shame, and game is transferable across denominations and traditions. For some, the Bible will be the whip by which leaders will create conformity and measure acceptance. Those under that perspective will find God to be vindictive and judgmental. For others, the primary tool will be the view of the community, the membership. Those who do not conform to the standards of the community will be blamed and shamed. Redemption comes only through the game. God is just as distant and uncaring, despite the rejection of concepts of judgment.

The narcissistic message looks very much the same whether it comes through the church, the business, the organization, or the family. No one measures up to the image; except, perhaps, the leader. All should be ashamed of their poor performance. The leadership offers a way of redemption through conformity and superior service.

In the church, this is the message of legalism. Those who perform well will be accepted. People are measured by their conduct. The only problem is that everyone continues to sin. No one meets the standard. Those who wish to be accepted will have to submit to the rules and guidance of the leadership.

In business, this is the message of performance. The employee who meets quota or expectations will be accepted, but the manager's job is to find what has been done wrong and bring it to the light. Employees under that kind of scrutiny will consistently fail. Negative marks on their records can be used later to explain the lack of a raise or promotion. Those who are faithful to attend the meetings and the seminars, who submit to criticisms and teaching, may be able to advance.

In the family, this is the message of conformity. The child who does what he is told will be accepted, but he may never please his father or mother. He fails again and again, no matter how hard he tries. Successful completion of a task results only in another task. But the child who causes few problems and cooperates with expectations may find reduced punishment and even praise, when mom or dad think it will motivate him toward greater responsibility.

In all of these, the narcissistic message rejects the person in favor of the image. Church members don't matter; employees don't matter; children don't matter. What matters is the goal, the ideal. If people get hurt as the organization or family pursues the image, that's too bad. It may look like narcissism and legalism are about performance management. The leaders in both manage the people for the sake of performance. Performance is measured, cultivated, and worshiped.

The truth is neither the message of legalism nor that of narcissism is about performance. When the standards are such that no one can reach perfection, the measurement of performance means nothing. If those who do very well are still infinitely far from the ideal, then there is little incentive for the rest who strive. The narcissist will not be content with consistently falling short of a goal, nor will the legalist be content with always being unacceptable. A different type of measurement must be encouraged, one which rewards both progress and effort. Rather than measure against the ideal, the new system will measure against others in the system.

In other words, those who strive under legalism no longer must measure up to Jesus (or to any ideal of a believer), but now

I don't have to be perfect, I just have to be better than you

are measured against other church members. I don't have to be perfect, we might say, I just have to be better than you. Success is having others believe you are better. Above average, superior, outstanding—these words are descriptions of achievement under that system. No longer is it about performance management. Now it is about *perception management*.

Perception management is not focused on shared standards, but on subjective measurements of chosen categories. To illustrate: those who rarely read their Bible would not compare with others on that basis. Instead, they would focus on clothing standards or holiday observances or involvement in politics. Others might compete in amount or type of television viewing. Some of the strange rules observed in church groups have come out of this desire to be better than others in something. Dietary restrictions (not for medical purposes), dress codes, hair length, speech patterns, loyalty to or avoidance of certain teachers, frequency of church attendance, place to sit during worship, schooling, prayer frequency and length—all of these and many more have been used to measure others.

Under the guise of spirituality, churches support certain types of behavior and reject others. Pastors and leaders promote the game by valuing certain behaviors in sermons and classes. They reward conformity to group standards with position and praise. Those who are perceived to be better within the system become models and leaders. Those perceived to be underachieving are scolded and marginalized.

A performance/perception system gives the legalist, by almost any definition, a way of measuring progress that is far more practical or worldly. As in any group, people measured against people have a greater opportunity to do well than those measured against an unforgiving standard. If others are struggling to do as well as I am, I can feel better about my rank without regard to how well I measure to the standard. One could be the "best" in the church without coming close to adequacy by the standard.

Narcissists are attracted to any comparison system that offers two things: rewards of status or power and opportunity to manipulate measurement of success. While most members of a legalist church or organization strive to be consistent in their performance for fear of being caught, the narcissist suffers no qualms about inconsistency. Because the narcissist has no real interest in performance, even spiritual performance, he/she can live one way at home and another at church or in public. While the legalist may wonder how he <u>did</u> in comparison to others, the narcissist will wonder how he <u>looked</u> in comparison to others. To reach the reward, the narcissist will not hesitate to lie to make himself look good and to make his "opponents" look bad. All that matters is reaching the reward.

We might wonder why church leadership would allow this type of system. There could be several reasons, including the fact that most were born and raised in a legalist environment. But a culture that promotes desired behavior without a reachable goal provides leadership a method of control. When people are bound to failure, they often submit to anyone who promises hope of acceptance. If leaders offer that hope, even with strings attached, they will have followers. Shifting the focus from one behavior to another will keep everyone off balance enough to maintain that control.

The Ever-shifting Goal

Apparently, it was Herbert Hoover, a president known more for his failures than his accomplishments, who said, "About the time we think we can make ends meet, somebody moves the ends." Hoover, of course, had the misfortune of being elected just before the beginning of the Great Depression. Perhaps depression is a logical consequence of ever-shifting ends. Humans are resourceful. Tell them what they are unable to do, and they will often find a way to do it. Set before them goals intended to keep them under control, and they may well find a way to surpass the goals and break the control. But give them goals that change and rules that are inconsistent, and they will become defeated.

One of the hallmarks of the narcissistic message is unclear expectations. People are told they do not measure up, but they must measure up. Rather than clear guidelines of how to measure up, they are given a variety of lists. Good Christians do this and avoid this. Good families act like this and not like that.

It would make sense if the narcissistic message sent people back to the Old Testament laws of Moses. At least that would seem to be Biblical. But the leaders who teach the message don't want to be accountable to those laws for themselves, nor do they want to do what the Law requires of leaders. So, they pick and choose from the laws. They call some "ceremonial" and others "moral." Most of the ceremonial laws are not for today, they say. Some of the moral laws are not for today, they say. Different teachers promote different laws.

And, of course, there are new laws. Certain activities are not for believers. Other activities are required for good Christians. Television, voting, dating, education—nearly every facet of daily life—all are regulated by some law from some leader. All are tied loosely to the Scriptures for full effect. But these rules change. They change according to the traditions or leadership of the church, but they also change over time. In fact, new laws can be added at any moment.

The following conversation is barely fictional. Two ladies meet at the park with their children. They have met at church, and they use this time to get to know each other. After the customary introductions and welcomes, this conversation begins.

A: Well, I was wondering, do you make your own bread for your family?

B: Why, yes, I do! Do you?

A: Oh, yes. That's the best. Do you grind your own wheat?

B: I sure do! And you?

A: Yes, that's the safest way. Do you make your own jellies?

B: Oh, yes, I love to make jelly! How about you?

A: I agree, that's the best way to control the sugars. And do you make your own butter?

B: Oh, uh, no. I don't make butter.

A: Oh. (Pause) Well, maybe I could teach you sometime.

Did you feel the rising hope of acceptance in B? Then the sudden and almost fatal drop? The standards seemed to be met, but then a new standard came in. When that one was met, another was found. Step by step… to failure. The conversation always ends with failure, because that's the goal. Blame must be discovered. Shame must be assigned. Only then will the victim be receptive to the leadership of the narcissist or the system. A's superiority is established. B's submission is expected. Of course, if B had done all that A asked about, another line of questions would have to begin. How many children? Do you make their clothing? Have you been to this or that conference? Have you followed this or that teacher? How much television do you watch? Questions might not be so direct, but a point of failure must be established. Once the failure is established, then the system begins to welcome the victim.

Some who claim to know say these are the tactics of cult groups, or groups that seek to control the thinking of their members. Acceptance and affirmation dangle like a carrot on a stick so the member is always striving, but never attaining. Eventually, the member wears out and becomes submissive. He/she will still do what is ordered but have no initiative. When the trap is realized, the victim is broken. Now the teacher and the system have control. The victim becomes grateful and dependent.

It is not difficult to see how these ever-shifting standards breed depression. Victims who are not overcome by the strategy cry out in pain. There seems to be no way to measure up. It is never enough. So many have shouted, "When will I ever be good enough?" But the narcissistic system, whether at church or work or home, has no interest in allowing people to be good enough. Those who reach the end slide out from under control.

The reason for the continual search for failure by managers, parents, and other leaders is control. Many managers believe employees must always feel the risk of losing their jobs in order to perform at their highest levels. Many parents think praising or thanking a child is simply being soft. Children should do what is expected. Praise is only allowed for performance above that which can be expected. Church leaders set the standards high because members must never lose sight of their unworthiness before God. Those who strive for holiness are reminded of the perfect holiness of the Savior, a goal which can never be reached by human effort. Their efforts, no matter how important for the Christian life, will never be enough.

When will I be good enough? That's the question asked by many church members. No matter how many conferences they have attended, how much Bible they have memorized, or how many hours of service they have suffered, they will never hear what they desire: "Well done, good and faithful servant. Enter into the joy of your Lord." At least, they will never hear it from the church. Some will be praised and honored as examples at their funerals, perhaps.

> When will I be good enough?

But there is little purpose, little benefit, to pronouncing people acceptable in this life. As long as they will strive harder, be more cooperative, or respect leaders more, the church will usually work to keep them feeling inadequate. If leaders can continue to come up with new ideas to offer as hope—steps to success—the people will be loyal and submissive. People who believe they are accepted are strong, and strong people can rebel. If the leaders can take away that confidence, make people believe they can never be certain about their acceptance, then order can be maintained.

Comparisons

Two men hiked in a forest one day and encountered a bear. The bear moved menacingly toward them. One of the men quickly reached into his backpack and took out his running shoes. As he started to change from his hiking boots, the other man said, "What are you doing? You'll never be able to outrun that bear!" The man with running shoes said, "I don't have to outrun the bear, I just have to outrun you!"

That old joke illustrates so well what we see happening in the narcissistic environment around us. Since no one can be as good as the ideal or the image, we only have to be better than the people to whom we will be compared. In church, the standard is Jesus. Almost by definition, no one can strive long enough or hard enough to be like Him. At work, employees are compared to the ideal worker, probably a figment of the manager's imagination. Since the ideal has never been defined, the manager may change his/her expectations.

The person in the narcissistic system may never reach the ideal, but he/she can be better than the others in the system. In fact, the person may never be as good as the leaders or the stars of the organization, but there are others with whom he/she can compare. As long as there is someone lower on the "totem pole," there is hope. As long as the member can be viewed as better than someone, there is a semblance of affirmation.

Some say every "only-child" should have a pet. When the boss yells at Dad, Dad comes home and yells at Mom. When Dad yells at Mom, Mom yells at Son. When Mom yells at Son, Son can yell at the dog. Those at the bottom, with no one to yell at, live sad and lonely lives. Obviously, that's tongue-in-cheek, but we understand.

Narcissists didn't come into the church to serve humbly. They came to rule. They came to be served. They came to be superior. In order to be superior, or to be recognized as superior, there must be people who are inferior. The narcissistic system, through its comparisons, creates inferior people.

Comparisons are the oil that allows the narcissistic machine to move. Without them, everyone would be stuck in their own shame. Since no amount of obedience or number of training events will overcome the blame, comparisons allow people to function. Every narcissistic system will function by comparisons. Churches have their star families; parents have their favorite child; work has its high performers. Not surprisingly, each also has someone on the other end of the spectrum. Every church has its fringe or marginal members. Every family has a black sheep. Every workplace has its underperformers. The lower a member is on the spectrum, the more thankful (and insecure) that person should be.

Yet, even the lowest members have their place. In fact, in some ways, their place is more secure than that of others. If they are willing to remain in the system, the system uses them to motivate the others. Many Christians grew up saying, "There, but for the grace of God, go I." For most, these are not words of

Comparisons are the oil that allows the narcissistic machine to move

compassion, but words of comparison. The Pharisee prayed and gave thanks that he was not a tax-collector. Even the lowest Pharisee, the one under discipline and rejected by all others, could say that. The tax collector could give thanks he was not born a woman. The woman could give thanks she was not born a slave. Every hierarchy needs someone on the bottom. We may think our culture has matured beyond such comparisons, but we deceive only ourselves. As long as performance/perception is the measure, there will be someone at the bottom. Psychologically, this is one of the strongest reasons for bigotry and prejudice.

While comparisons can be part of any group, the church certainly seems made for them. Since we cannot achieve perfection, we compare ourselves with each other. Our denomination is better than others. Our church is the best church. Our small group is the most faithful. Our family is superior. I try harder than others. We pick and choose Scripture and doctrines to make ourselves feel good about our status. We use comparisons to lift ourselves up, to put others down, and to motivate ourselves to work harder.

The only problem is that comparisons are self-defeating. Wherever a person stands in a comparison system, it cannot be high enough to avoid competition. And where there is competition, there is the possibility of failure. The president of the United States, the Pope, the kings of various lands, all these positions have been challenged and overthrown. It may be as gentle as being voted out of office, or it may be as violent as assassination. Those at the highest levels of management function knowing their jobs are less secure than the part-time employees at the bottom of the business hierarchy. It's not just lonely at the top, it's dangerous.

We shake our heads at the beauty queen who stands in front of the mirror crying because of her imperfections. We wonder at the record-holding athletes who push themselves to the breaking point to stay ahead of others. We grieve for the young person who commits suicide because she listens to the social media bullying. How is it possible, we ask, that these who have so much going for them can feel so worthless. Comparisons hurt...and sometimes kill.

We ought to ask how it became possible the church embraced the narcissistic system that uses comparisons to control and manipulate. Surely the Lord who loves us would not establish such a system. So much division and abuse has come out of the church. There must be something better.

The Gospel

Many Christians reading this will wonder if there is any other way. The narcissistic message has so pervaded the church that it is difficult to see anything else. Some give up on church. They reject everything the church stands for. In anger and grief and frustration, they seek acceptance outside the church. Others just give up. They attend worship services expecting nothing and finding it. They have abandoned hope of measuring up to any standard. They try not to think about forgiveness and future hope, because their hearts are so damaged from the bait-and-switch spirituality of their church. They attend to see their friends, to participate in a community, to cling to some possibility of hope for acceptance. Many, of course, are still playing the game. They live with their blame and shame and strive to be better than others. They dream of being noticed for their efforts and forgiven for their failures. For them, this is the only way.

But there is another way. Yes, a better way. A way to find acceptance and peace in spite of your failures and weaknesses. A way of freedom and joy for your heart. That way is Jesus.

The Christian gospel has never been about performance. How well you behave or perform has never been the real question. Churches and church leaders might have focused on how much people give or serve or how obedient they are, but that is not the message of the gospel. In fact, the message of the gospel and the narcissistic message are opposites.

We open the door to narcissistic abuse by being aware of our inadequacies. We struggle against limitations and failure all our lives. We have learned to define ourselves by our deficiencies. The narcissist comes to convince us of his superiority, and we accept him because we want to believe we could be superior as well. We accept because we want to be accepted. The narcissistic system thrives because it offers us the hope of climbing some ladder of success. The less we find success, the more we seek acceptance and comfort from those who will use us for their own benefit.

The Christian gospel accepts our failure, of which we are so aware, as a statement of fact. There is no false hope that we could become better by working harder or identifying with those who lie to us. We have all sinned, the Scriptures teach. All, from the greatest to the least, according to whatever system you have accepted. All have sinned. All have failed. And all need a Savior.

While the narcissistic message tells you how you have failed and must strive—without hope—to do better, the message of the gospel acknowledges your failure and need and leads you to the One who is good enough. The message of law and work and pain must yield to the message of love. As Paul says, we are no longer under law, but under grace. It is the grace of God that shows us His love.

All the promises of forgiveness and eternal life are based on identification, rather than performance. Those who come to Jesus find forgiveness in Him. Those who come to Jesus for new life find that life in Him. Eternal life is in Him because He is eternal. We are in Him, and He is in us. The gospel is a message about identification with Jesus.

There is little attraction for the narcissist to the real message of the gospel because there is no opportunity to claim superiority. If all have sinned and failure is endemic, then all equally need a Savior. No one can claim spiritual superiority if all are dependent on the same Person for their spirituality. No one can be more righteous if our only righteousness comes from Jesus. If our need was equal, and it was, and the gift is equal, and it is, then, in Christ we are all equal. One Savior gave one life to offer salvation to all.

From the custodian to the Pope, from the most pious preacher to the drunk, all must be covered with the blood of Jesus to be saved. All come to the cross with nothing and leave with everything. It is the same for everyone. This is not a message the legalist can use to keep people in line. This is not a message the narcissist can twist to make others praise or obey him. This is a message of acceptance and love in Jesus alone.

Those who know they are accepted are strong. The more certain they are of their acceptance in Jesus, the less they are open to manipulation or control by others. They are dangerous people, as far as the narcissistic system is concerned. There is true freedom and power in the gospel of Jesus.

Conclusion

This is a book about narcissism. It is not intended to be an indictment of the church. Our Lord established the church, even local fellowships, for our good. It is His intent to use the church to bless His people and move His kingdom forward.

However, when the members and leaders of the church have been deceived into comparisons and hierarchies and legalistic performance, the church has offered a haven for abusers. That haven has been so desirable that many churches and denominations have become narcissistic organizations, often led by narcissists. When we understand not all narcissism is overt and loud, that some manipulate from more protected positions, then we can recognize the touch of the narcissistic hand in many of the abuses, marginalizations, and prejudices some have suffered in church.

Some writers and professionals dismiss the idea of narcissistic abuse by saying we are all narcissists to some degree. It is natural, they say, for some to use narcissistic techniques more often and/or more harshly. But, they say, we cannot judge those who do so, because we are like them only to a lesser degree. There are two fallacies in this. First, it may be that narcissistic behavior is a natural part of the human flesh, but the life-changing power of the gospel and even the guiding pressure of human society move most people away from that behavior.

Most people are simply not narcissists. They may exhibit similar behaviors at lesser levels, but their behavior does not fit the definitions of narcissism. It may be that envy is similar in root to thievery, but envying is not the same as stealing. We punish only the act that harms others, not the thoughts or desires that are hindered by whatever moral pressure is applied.

In the same way, it is not inevitable that churches should be narcissistic. Certainly not all pastors or church leaders are narcissists. Most live generous and sacrificial lives. Most pastors sincerely care about the people they serve and the message they bring. We tend to hear about those who use the church to serve themselves. We certainly remember them if they have affected our lives. Nor do narcissistic pastors always leave behind narcissistic churches. The foundation of love and mission may often be strong enough to overcome the damage done by narcissists.

It is not inevitable that churches should be narcissistic

The second fallacy is connected to the first. If it is true that the seeds of narcissism are in all of us, but most of us do not submit to the temptations or copy the behaviors, then it is entirely appropriate for us to notice (judge, if you will) those who give in to the dark desires. The idea that we are not to judge, since we are believers, or that we cannot judge, because we suffer the same temptations, is nonsense. The same Scriptures that warn us against judging others tell us to admonish evildoers, avoid sinful acts, and administer justice. It would be impossible to do these things without making some judgment about another person's behavior. I may not be able to tell whether a person is saved, but I can tell if that person's behaviors hurt others. Eternal condemnation is not in my jurisdiction, but I am called to evaluate and condemn certain behaviors. Narcissistic abuse should be called out and stopped wherever possible.

And believers should be free to challenge or leave narcissistic churches and organizations. Leaders and members can be called to account for behavior. The only question is whether such accounting will be profitable. Those who suffer in narcissistic or abusive relationships may, and perhaps should, leave if possible. Those who try to stay in the relationship will find it is not possible to change a narcissist who doesn't see anything wrong with his/her behaviors. Participation in a local church or organization is voluntary. If the group exhibits narcissistic behaviors, those who do not wish to remain should be free to go. Changing an organization or church that has begun to serve an image at the expense of its members will be very difficult, perhaps not possible.

Then there are those who say we should not call people or organizations narcissistic at all, that the term should be left to the professionals who diagnose personality disorders. There is no attempt in this book to label certain people with a clinical disorder, nor even to define a clinical term in a new way. The idea of narcissism as a popular description of certain behaviors and values is well established. It is not inappropriate for us to use some designation to refer to this type of abuser. If the term, narcissist, is thought to be improper, another can be used. But using that term to describe those who act or think in accordance with the clinical definitions of narcissism is not out of line.

If, as some suggest, our culture is becoming more narcissistic, then the church should be first a place of refuge and then a place of change. Victims of manipulation and depersonalization should find the church to be welcoming and helpful. Those who abuse should find the church to be a place where their behavior is exposed and confronted.

What does it mean for us to be salt and light in the world if not to stand against this pervasive and destructive evil called narcissism?

And what does it mean for us to be separate from the world if not to be separate from this hurtful behavior and culture?

Options

So, what are you supposed to do if the church you attend shows signs of having yielded to narcissism? What is a victim of narcissistic abuse in a family or a marriage supposed to do if the church supports the narcissist? Where can victims or concerned believers go to avoid or escape the narcissistic mindset?

Many have simply found another church. Not all churches are narcissistic. If you have felt marginalized or victimized in a large church, a smaller church may offer closer relationships and relief from the constant marketing and striving. If you have found a small church to be just a more confining setting for narcissistic abuse, perhaps a larger church would offer a less pressured opportunity for worship. Churches of the same denomination may differ greatly, and you may find a different denomination to be a refreshing change.

As you read the above, you realize that narcissistic abuse can happen in almost any church. Some have felt it necessary to leave the church altogether. They cannot help connecting the things of the faith to the abuse they have suffered. Or they have continued to believe but apart from the organized church.

213

There is a growing movement of believers who gather with other believers for times of prayer and singing and even learning without any connection to a church. This "unchurching" movement encourages people to connect with others at times outside the traditional Sunday morning service. Some even continue to use that time slot but meet in living rooms and side rooms of coffee shops. The point is to set aside the structure of the institutional church while returning to the culture of the church as first conceived. Without a hierarchy to maintain or a denomination to service, these small groups have the potential of ministering, teaching, and even disciplining in loving Biblical ways. A few churches even encourage this kind of fellowship, training and commissioning members to reach out to neighbors and friends without the goal of bringing more people to the church services.

Be reminded, however, that narcissists can creep into small groups just as easily as large ones. You and I might think the size would discourage manipulators and controllers, but that doesn't seem to be the case. Small fellowships often find themselves led by narcissists.

Just be diligent. Knowing these abusers are out there, learning what they want and do, will help you to see it happening. If you can't stop it, leave it. But understand that wherever two or three are gathered, the narcissist sees an opportunity. You are smarter and stronger now. Hold to the principles of love and acceptance. Reject the hierarchies and pedestals. Value the lowest as you do the highest, whatever that means in your group. And, if you see a narcissist beginning to manipulate, call him/her out. If the narcissist wins, as they often do, move on.

Perhaps the answer is to be willing to bend tradition a little. Seek, the Lord said, and you shall find. If you would like to meet with other believers apart from the narcissistic message, look for the opportunity. There are others looking as well.

Addenda

(The following articles are answers to some of the more common and pertinent questions I have received regarding narcissism in a Christian context.)

The Changed Narcissist

What would a changed narcissist look like? I have had many people write to ask me whether a narcissist could change. I have also had narcissists write to me to tell me they have changed. In fact, I have been criticized for not trusting the changed narcissist.

But I have also heard many stories of spouses and others who have opened their doors and their hearts to their narcissist again—on the promise of change—only to find that the problems in the relationship increased. The victim finally gets up the courage to set boundaries or to separate, and the narcissist gets the message. Change or else. So, the narcissist changes. If he hit, he stops hitting. If she criticized, she stops criticizing. If the narcissist was demanding or demeaning or whatever, the behavior stops. Then he/she wants to be welcomed back to the relationship. After all, look at all the change.

That story is common. Sadly. But what happens behind the scenes is also common, just not as obvious. Narcissists are political deal makers. Over and over I hear that the narcissist has gone to friends to convince them that he has changed. Then the friends go to the victim to try to convince her. Behind the scenes, the narcissist has planted the idea that she is the real problem. Yes, he has done some wrong things, but it takes two. If she would only open up, he could show her he has changed. So, the "friends" (or pawns) begin their play.

The same thing often happens when the narcissist goes to the church leaders. The pastor or counselor or elder hears the narcissist's story and is then set against the victim. By the time the victim goes for counsel, the stage is already set. Sometimes the abuse victim goes to the pastor only to find out he has already been "working with" the abuser.

Involving friends or family or even outsiders is evidence the narcissist has really not changed. That's just politics. The deal-making is evident as the narcissist only changes the things that have been issues. If the victim talked mostly about lying, he will be overly truthful. If the victim pointed out the abuse, the abuse will stop. But little else will change. Only the things that must change in order to restore the relationship. Just the minimum.

The political deal-maker sees a relationship as a negotiated partnership. He offers his part, and you offer yours. He will promise to do what you want, and you will promise to do what he wants. When the deal-maker is a narcissist, your part will be the only one with substance. In other words, he will say he has changed, and you are supposed let him live with you again. Notice the inequality of that deal?

This is the personal equivalent of the "we have to pass the bill before we can read it" scenario. (For those who have no idea what that means, it refers to legislation that is pushed through by one side without opportunity for the other side to examine the bill. Yes, that's American politics. But it is also narcissistic politics.) You must give in order to see if the other side is being honest. That's why it isn't until the narcissist is back and settled that you realize he/she had no intention of keeping the promise.

And once the narcissist is settled, the deal is done. There is little reason to continue the change. In fact, because you have spent your resources and resolve, he/she will become even more abusive. He has established himself as the real victim to the friends and the real victor to you. It will be harder for you to find the strength to break the relationship next time.

Now, this story is surprisingly common. It is also surprising to me how many have had the courage to go through all this a second time (or a third). The victims finally learned how the game was played, and they stopped negotiating.

By the way, this doesn't happen only in marriages. This could be co-workers or friends or family members. It could be a compromised pastor. If the narcissist needs you, he/she will adjust behavior to try to make you believe in the change.

Yes, narcissists can adjust their behavior. They don't treat everyone the same. They adjust their behavior depending on what their goal is. They don't treat you like they treated you at the beginning of the relationship. The narcissist can control behavior. That's just one of the things that makes me suggest narcissistic abuse is a choice, rather than an illness.

I have also suggested that changed behavior may be an acceptable goal if the desire for change is real and the change is enforced. Boundaries and counseling can help the narcissist learn to function in a relationship. If the cost of losing the relationship is significant in the narcissist's mind, negotiation might make a difference. Some spouses (or others) may accept that in order to provide stability for the family or mutual benefit in the relationship.

But real and enforced change is usually not what the narcissist offers when he wants back into the relationship. That's a longer process, and most narcissists will not be interested.

I wrote about narcissists who claim they have changed so their spouses will welcome them back into the relationship. Many sad stories have come from those who have fallen for that deception. Of course, there is no foolproof way to determine if someone has changed or if that person is just playing a game. But it seems to me there are some things that would indicate real change.

So, what would a changed narcissist look like? The following points are about a male narcissist who wants to return to his wife. We all understand that some women are narcissists and that not all narcissistic relationships are in marriages. Adjust these as you see fit.

1. He finally understands it is not all about him. Narcissists will talk about their needs, their efforts, their pain, their loneliness, their revelations, their decisions, their inconveniences. But they will not talk about you or your needs. The broken relationship has been a burden on them, but they don't acknowledge how the relationship was a burden on you. They will tell you over and over how they have changed, how they accept your anger, and how they are struggling to be alone. All about them. Is it a struggle for you to be alone? Are you struggling with your anger? Do you have rights and expectations in the relationship? The narcissist doesn't talk about that because he doesn't think about that.

   When the narcissist can honestly see and admit how he has hurt you, then he may be changing. When he finally stops thinking about his own struggle and sees yours as valid, then maybe change is happening.

2. He begins to think about what he can give, rather than what he can get. The narcissist makes deals. He expresses what he wants, and you are supposed to do it. He may not even realize there should be another side to the deal. And, when he does, you don't know if he will fulfill his side. As long as the narcissist is bargaining, he is manipulating. What if he stopped making deals? What if he just gave, like a loving

person would? When he gives you more money than agreed upon because he knows you can use it, even when it makes the month tight for him, he may be changing. When he takes care of chores you need (not chores he needs or likes), because he knows you need them, maybe he is changing.

3. He stops blaming you for the break-up. Narcissists are experts at blaming the victim. Their whole game is to make themselves look good. That will mean you have to be the one who caused the problem. That's what they think, and that's what they will tell others. Eventually, you may begin to believe it. Once you do, he wins. Now, if he stops talking about what you should do to change and sees his own failures, then maybe he is changing. If he comes to the relationship without trying to make a deal where you have to give something or give up something, then change might be happening. If he openly and honestly discusses what he did to hurt you, and accepts it from your point of view, then maybe.

4. He goes back to friends and tells them the truth. There is little doubt that the narcissist has already talked to friends about what you have done. He probably did it long before you began to see the truth about him. Certainly, once you started talking about separation, he tried to get them on his side. Now he should go back to them and tell them it was his fault, not yours. He should admit to them that he is manipulative and controlling and that he has hurt you. At minimum, he should speak supportively about you. If he were to do this, maybe he is changing.

5. He's willing to take time. Restoring the relationship is about winning your heart again. Is he willing to take the time, to proceed gently, to do that? Does he assume certain privileges because he has had them before? Some narcissists simply do not accept that you are committed to separation. They think they just have to say the right words or make the right deal and you will yield. They search for the magic answer, so all this will stop. If he is patient, maybe he is changing. If he puts the relationship at such a value that he is willing to take time, perhaps even years, to bring it together again, maybe he is changing.

6. He's willing to lose. Most narcissistic relationships end when the narcissist says they do. Many end because he finds someone else. Others end because "she is unreasonable." They will redecorate the story until it is your fault. Whatever it takes to win. Narcissists must win. Their image cannot afford to lose. But if he is willing to do what you want, because you want it, maybe he is changing. I have known men who lost their marriages and blame themselves. No, they were not narcissists, at least from what I could see. But they would tell you there was a time in their marriage when they were selfish and abusive and lost the best thing they ever had. They understand why the person they hurt is better off without them. Bottom line: they were jerks and they lost. If the narcissist is willing to accept that, then maybe he is changing.

By the way, going online to tell as many as will listen how much suffering you have caused, even when you seem to blame yourself, is just another way to win. Becoming the "expert" on narcissistic relationships because you are one, may be a victory in itself. If he is blogging about his struggle or counseling others, he may have found a different way to come out ahead.

7. He's no longer angry. Change is hard, but kindness and understanding are patient. We can understand frustration when there is one goal and it isn't happening. But if the above things are in place, and the narcissist is kind and not angry (over time), then maybe real change is taking place. If there is anything that makes narcissists angry, it is you pointing out their failures by setting boundaries or separating. They get frustrated when they cannot find those magic words or manipulate you into changing your mind. They watch the clock and/or the calendar waiting for "all this" to be over, then get angry when it takes time. If the anger has stopped, maybe he is changing.

Beware of the anger adapting. Anger can change to resignation. Shrugging his shoulders and saying "whatever" may be just a different way of expressing anger. The "sad sack," the defeated victim, can manipulate in much the same way as the angry person. Don't be fooled. There is a difference between honestly acknowledging your failure and becoming a broken-down moping servant.

Some will respond that this is ridiculous. "No one could possibly do all of these things. You are suggesting the narcissist

go completely soft, take all the blame, and become a doormat."
Well, perhaps I am. Perhaps this list is tough with expectations
that are high. But they are not too high for regular people, people
who do stupid things and want to rebuild their relationships.
Nothing on the list above is unreasonable. Yet, I acknowledge
they might be difficult. I also acknowledge they are inconsistent
with narcissism.

Is Change Possible?

I was recently accused of teaching that narcissists never change, that change is impossible. I know many people believe this to be true, but I do not. Instead, I have taught that narcissists rarely change—because they don't think anything is wrong with them.

There are several factors in determining whether a person can change his or her narcissistic behavior. We must acknowledge that there is a spectrum of this abusive behavior. We also must remember that we use the term "narcissist" in a popular sense, rather than as a professional diagnosis. I don't know if someone who is diagnosed as a narcissist by a psychologist is capable of real change. Some, like Wendy Behary, claim to have success working with these folks. I am not a credentialed psychological professional, and I do not work with diagnosed narcissists. Here we talk about those users and manipulators more popularly called narcissists.

We also have to distinguish between the behavior of the narcissist and the heart of the narcissist. I don't know if the narcissist can change his/her heart. It may be possible, with enough motivation. Yet, since narcissists value others and relationships so lowly, I would be hard-pressed to know what that motivation would be. (There is a way to change the heart, of course, and I write about that below.)

I do know narcissists can change their behavior. As I have said before, they do it all the time. With motivation, they can stop abusing. Good counselors can help them learn to live kindly with others. They may even learn not to be afraid of losing whatever they are protecting. If they can learn not to hurt others, and if those others have relatively low expectations for heart connections, then I would think narcissists could change sufficiently to restore relationships.

We forget that many marriages of the past were functional relationships. Today we seem to think marriage partners should always be "in love," meaning romantically infatuated. Not only was that not a requirement for most of history, it is not necessarily the primary goal for marriage today. With children and property and work involved, a good marriage can just be one where the couple gets along as good friends. No, I am not suggesting that should be enough for everyone, but I am saying that can be a satisfying and legitimate relationship for some. So, changing from narcissistic behavior to kind and cooperative behavior might work for some relationships. I do think many of those we think of as narcissists could make that change if they wanted.

But to love? That's the real question. Could the narcissist learn to love? If narcissists have difficulty in relationships because they don't know how to love, or are unable, then how could that change? It would take a new heart.

I only know one way to get a new heart.

> *I will give you a new heart and put a new spirit within you; I will take the heart of stone out of your flesh and give you a heart of flesh. Ezekiel 36:26*

There is a way to get a heart that feels and cares. There is a way to get a living heart able to connect with others. A new heart that both receives and gives love. That heart comes from Jesus. That heart comes when His life is exchanged for yours.

I know we all wonder if a narcissist can be a Christian. One of my favorite passages of Scripture directly addresses this.

> *Do you not know that the unrighteous will not inherit the kingdom of God? Do not be deceived. Neither fornicators, nor idolaters, nor adulterers, nor homosexuals, nor sodomites, nor thieves, nor covetous, nor drunkards, nor revilers, nor extortioners will inherit the kingdom of God. And such were some of you. But you were washed, but you were sanctified, but you were justified in the name of the Lord Jesus and by the Spirit of our God. 1 Corinthians 6:9-11*

So, if someone was a narcissist and came to Jesus for salvation, that person is no longer a narcissist. He/she may act like a narcissist, but the identity has been washed away and victory is possible. The behavior may remain, just as much of our old behavior continued after conversion, but that behavior can be changed. Ex-narcissists can learn not to do what narcissists do, just like ex-thieves can learn not to do what thieves do—and be free of the evil motivations—because of the new heart in Jesus.

I cannot say whether your narcissist is a Christian. All I can say is a real Christian is both able and motivated to change. I can also say no heart change is possible without Jesus. If your narcissist has never truly submitted to Jesus, come to Him for new life, then the best that can happen is some changed behavior. So, when a narcissist contacts me, that's where we go. I place the challenges of changed behavior and heart motivation before them and invite them to new life in Jesus.

To summarize: a narcissist can change some behavior, but not his/her heart. Only Jesus can change the heart.

The Christian Narcissist

All the narcissists I have known have been Christians.

Now, there are a couple of things that must go along with that statement. First, I mean they consider themselves Christians and they want everyone else to consider them Christians. Second, I don't get out much.

I have been asked several times to write something on the Christian Narcissist. I must admit that I find that designation to be troubling. It seems like an oxymoron, a term that has contradictory parts. I am tempted to say there cannot be such a creature, yet I do know people who might seem to fit. In fact, many churches have them. So, here's what I know:

Christians are people saved by Jesus. They draw their life from Him and could draw their behavior from His Spirit. But they often, perhaps usually, draw their behavior from the patterns that developed throughout their early life. In other words, sometimes we act like Christians and sometimes we don't. That's true of all of us.

Narcissism is a flesh pattern that developed in early life and became the coping mechanism of choice in handling the stresses of life. This happened while the person was very young and has been reinforced constantly throughout life. That means if such a person would become a believer he or she would almost certainly continue to struggle with narcissistic behavior in relationships.

Narcissistic behavior can be seen in almost anyone and appears in society as a continuum. Those who practice it intuitively (without thinking) and regularly—to the detriment of their relationships—are the ones we label as narcissists.

Those whose behavior and values warrant being designated as narcissists are unwilling or unable to care about others in normal ways and tend to use others in their process of handling life. They think of little other than how to manipulate people in ways that benefit themselves or serve the image of themselves they want to promote.

Narcissism is contrary to the Christian faith. Because the narcissist will not admit failure or need, in order to protect the image, he or she will also not admit sinfulness or unworthiness and will not see the need for repentance or brokenness. Those who receive Christ as life, do so as they understand their own failure and need. Narcissists would find it very difficult to do this.

However, Christian behavior is easy to fake and many in the church are naive and gullible and are particularly vulnerable to the manipulations and deceit of the narcissist. The church is a prime hunting ground for narcissists, with little real accountability and significant opportunity for attention and promotion.

Narcissists are able and willing to adapt their behavior and words for the purpose of promoting their image and will use organizations, such as the church, to accomplish their goals.

So, what do I take from all of this? That none of us should be surprised to find narcissists in church! Are they Christians? That isn't mine to say. While narcissism is contrary to Christ, narcissistic behavior may be just old flesh patterns at work in the life of the believer. People who exhibit these characteristics will almost always be successful in persuading most of the people to accept and honor them, usually because the majority of the people won't spend enough time to see the truth.

But what do you do about it? Protect yourself. Learn to recognize the behavior that hurts you and others. You probably will not be able to change the minds of church leadership toward the narcissist. They are often the last ones to see the damage these folks can do. If you must call attention to their actions, be sure to point out the behavior, rather than the motivation. Tell what they do. Maybe you can help others by pointing out what you see or by coming alongside victims when they are hurt.

I wish there was a more helpful and effective way of dealing with narcissists, particularly in the church. But the truth is these people usually win. They are ruthless, willing to use whatever information and opportunities they are given to defend themselves and attack those who threaten them. Most of the time it just isn't worth it. Churches and volunteer organizations are poorly prepared to deal with predators of any kind. It would probably be better just to find another church.

Can a Narcissist be Saved?

Yes, I think it is possible for a narcissist to be saved. Narcissism, even in a professional diagnosis, is not easily defined. It presents as a continuum. Some are more narcissistic than others; some exhibit more of one characteristic and less of another; some may become more narcissistic in certain situations. So, the person you and I might consider an example of narcissism may simply be at some point on the continuum, a point that particularly affects us. I am not suggesting that a "diagnosis" of narcissism is arbitrary, but it does seem to be true that different people see a narcissist differently.

I wouldn't presume to be able to decide at what point a person no longer can see his or her need for a Savior. It would be difficult to find a more extreme example of narcissism than Ted Bundy, the serial murderer. Yet, Dr. James Dobson believed Bundy responded to the gospel and opened his heart to the Lord. It is hard for me to believe, but I know the love of Christ is available to all, no matter what the sins have been, and that love is enough for anyone. Could Ted Bundy have understood his own life was about to end and he could no longer hide from the truth? Could he have finally admitted he needed forgiveness and life? No matter how unlikely it seems, I suppose it is possible.

Many believers relate how the Lord took them to a place of brokenness, a place where they finally understood life didn't work their way. That brokenness can range from an overwhelming sense of need to the actual loss of almost everything the person believed was important. The flesh, which is the system we create to control life and make it safe for ourselves, stands against the Spirit of God. When the futility of the flesh becomes so obvious, the heart becomes open finally to the Spirit. Even if the flesh pattern is what we have called narcissism, this process is possible.

It is right to ask the question, however. The very definition of narcissism includes the unwillingness to allow that brokenness. Lack of control, weakness, acceptance of failure— these are the things the narcissist avoids at almost any cost. It seems like it would be most difficult for a person like this to repent, but maybe those are the cases where the love of God is strongest.

Resources

The following list is a small, but significant, representation of the books available on narcissism and church abuse. These have been a great help to me as I studied the issue over the past several years. There are many books today on this subject. Those who are interested in studying it with a layperson's perspective should find these a good place to begin.

A Cry for Justice

Jeff Crippen's book is about abuse in the context of the church: how it happens and how it finds support. Through many examples, Crippen leads the reader to practical understanding and solutions. If you want your church to be a refuge for the hurting, read this book. Jeff is no longer with the ministry named in the title but can be found at unholycharade.com.

Crippen, Jeff and Anna Wood. A Cry for Justice. Calvary Press, 2012.

Children of the Self-absorbed
Working with the Self-absorbed

Nina Brown is widely considered one of the leading authorities on narcissistic abuse in relationships. These two books are an excellent place to begin a study of narcissism in parental and work relationships.

Brown, Nina. Children of the Self-Absorbed. Oakland: New Harbinger Publications, 2001.

Brown, Nina. Working with the Self-absorbed. Oakland: New Harbinger Publications, 2002.

Disarming the Narcissist

Wendy Behary is a counselor and teacher who works with narcissists. Although this book has more to do with how victims may cope in narcissistic relationships, she reveals the types of therapy used in working with self-absorbed or narcissistic people.

Behary, Wendy. Disarming the Narcissist. Oakland: New Harbinger Publications, 2008.

Not Under Bondage: Biblical Divorce for Abuse, Adultery and Desertion

This carefully written book should be on the shelf of every pastor and counselor who deals with people in abusive marriages and struggles with applying the teachings of Scripture to these troubling situations. Roberts is currently the director of A Cry for Justice.

Roberts, Barbara. Not Under Bondage. Maschil Press, 2008.

The Narcissistic Family

The Pressmans have provided a scholarly, but understandable, overview of the effect of narcissistic abuse within the family.

Donaldson-Pressman, Stephanie and Robert M. Pressman. The Narcissistic Family. San Francisco: Josey-Bass, 1994.

Unchurching: Christianity without Churchianity

Do you have to attend an institutional church with its politics and positioning? Richard Jacobson and the thousands who have embraced the *Unchurching* movement don't think so. They gather with other believers to praise the Lord and study the Word apart from the structures and strictures of traditional churches.

Jacobson, Richard. Unchurching. Unchurching Books, 2016.

The Wizard of Oz and Other Narcissists

One of the more popular books on narcissism and the struggle of victims. Payson is a marriage and family counselor.

Payson, Eleanor D. The Wizard of Oz and Other Narcissists. Royal Oak, MI: Julian Day Publications, 2002.

Made in the USA
Middletown, DE
20 August 2022

71740095R00136